M. A. C. K.

Tactics

● ●

The Science of Seduction
Meets the Art of Hostage Negotiation

Rob Wiser
and
Christopher Curtis

Roadside Amusements
an imprint of Chamberlain Bros.
a member of Penguin Group (USA) Inc.
New York
2005

ROADSIDE AMUSEMENTS
an imprint of
CHAMBERLAIN BROS.
Published by the Penguin Group
Penguin Group (USA) Inc., 375 Hudson Street, New York, New York 10014, USA
Penguin Group (Canada), 90 Eglinton Avenue East, Suite 700, Toronto, Ontario
M4P 2Y3, Canada (a division of Pearson Penguin Canada Inc.)
Penguin Books Ltd, 80 Strand, London WC2R 0RL, England
Penguin Ireland, 25 St Stephen's Green, Dublin 2, Ireland
(a division of Penguin Books Ltd)
Penguin Group (Australia), 250 Camberwell Road, Camberwell, Victoria 3124,
Australia (a division of Pearson Australia Group Pty Ltd)
Penguin Books India Pvt Ltd, 11 Community Centre, Panchsheel Park,
New Delhi–110 017, India
Penguin Group (NZ), Cnr Airborne and Rosedale Roads, Albany, Auckland 1310,
New Zealand (a division of Pearson New Zealand Ltd)
Penguin Books (South Africa) (Pty) Ltd, 24 Sturdee Avenue, Rosebank,
Johannesburg 2196, South Africa

Penguin Books Ltd, Registered Offices: 80 Strand, London WC2R 0RL, England

Illustrations by TK

Library of Congress Cataloging-in-Publication Data

Wiser, Rob.
    M.A.C.K. tactics: the science of seduction meets the art of hostage negotiation /
Rob Wiser and Christopher Curtis.
        p.   cm.
    ISBN 1-59609-167-3
    1. Dating (Social customs).   2. Seduction.   3. Man-woman relationships.
    4. Single men—Life skills guides.   I. Title: M.A.C.K. tactics.   II. Curtis,
Christopher.   III. Title.
    HQ801.W76   2005   2005048485
    646.7'7'081—dc22

Printed in the United States of America
1 3 5 7 9 10 8 6 4 2

Book design by Elke Sigal

Acknowledgments

Rob Wiser wishes to thank:

Peter Miller, Julie Hahn, Anna Cowles, Carlo DeVito, CT Tamura, Trevor Agar, Mike McKeever, Cathryn Jaymes, Adam Fine, Annabelle Fortin, Ronen Olshansky, James "Big Jim" Reardon, Alex Wiser, and Bob Wiser.

And a very special thanks to my mom, the extraordinary Sheila Reardon, whose love, perseverance, and support will always inspire my writing.

Christopher Curtis wishes to thank:

God, my pops Bernard Curtis for always being a man, li'l sis Doren, Shawn Brown, Amaze, John Ewing, Ayelet Roth, Salvatore Mascoli, Cathryn James for always believing, Eric Nelson, Sean Clary, Rafique Waddell, Big Swoo, my squad Northeast 33, L. J. Hansen, the entire staff at PMA and the Big Lion Peter, everyone at Steve Madden, and every woman who ever told me no (for making me try harder).

And above all, the woman who holds me down no matter what: Dorothy Duckett, my beautiful mother.

Contents

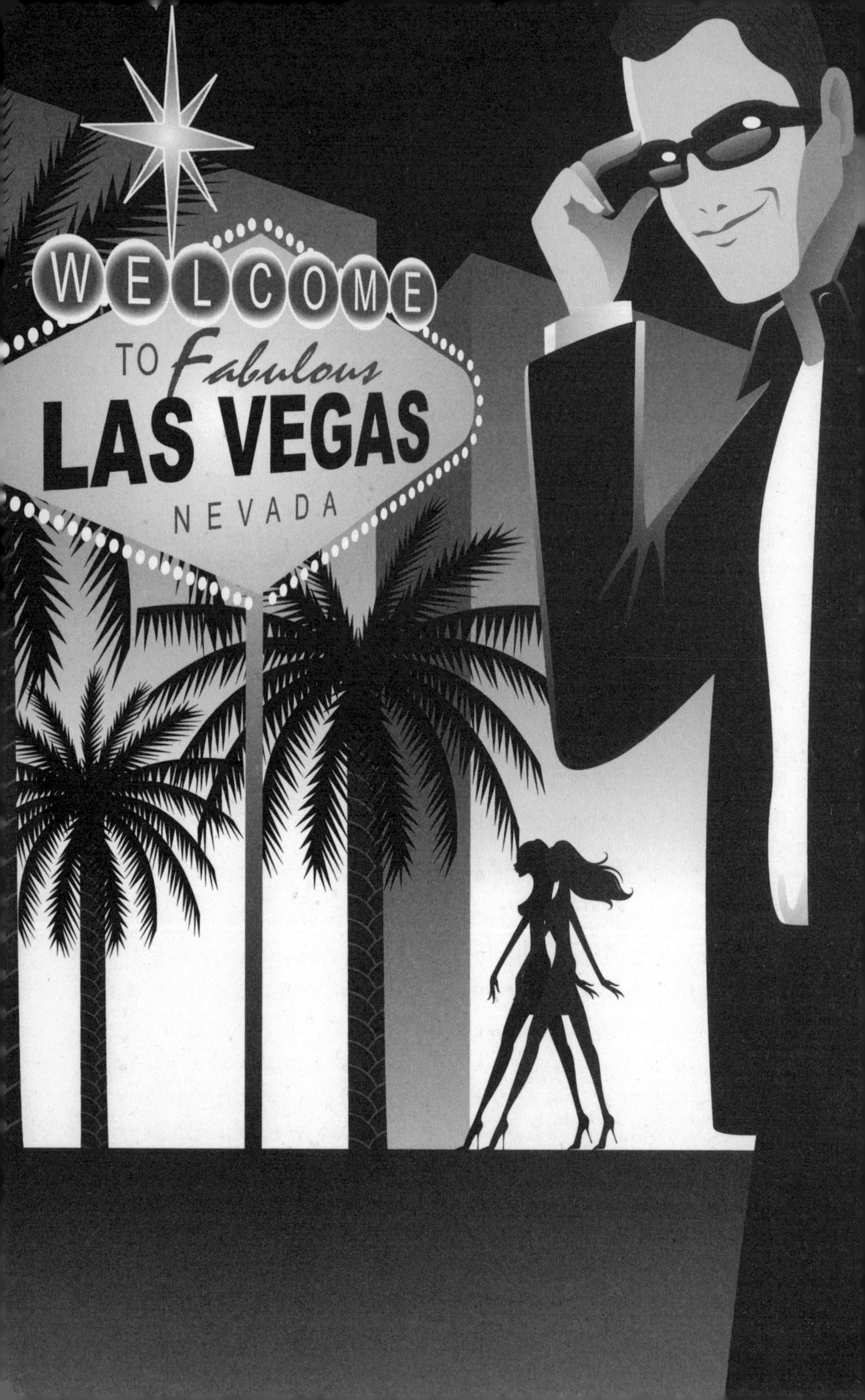
WELCOME
TO Fabulous
LAS VEGAS
NEVADA

Introduction

So there I was, a recent transplant from New York City living in Las Vegas. The city that *truly* never sleeps. Forget the gambling and the glitz for a minute; anyone who's partied here knows this is the land of beautiful, knee-weakening women, a mind-boggling cross section of babes from across the country and every corner of the globe.

But I was hesitant about jumping into this game. I'd always done respectably with the opposite sex, but a recent breakup had left me disillusioned with dating and wary of women. My confidence was in a slump. I felt like I didn't understand what women wanted; I wasn't even sure what *I* wanted.

Then, one night at a casino bar, a Christopher Curtis introduced himself. Normally I have no interest in striking up a conversation with another guy at four in the morning, but I could immediately sense there was something extraordinary about him. He carried himself with confidence, yet he had an extremely friendly, likable vibe. I was surprised when he mentioned he was a police officer, due to his colorful tattoos and hipster clothes. Then again, it explained his remarkable ability to read and communicate with people.

Ten minutes later, you would have thought we were a couple of old college buddies—smiling and sharing stories about the one subject guys are invariably going to discuss at four in the morning. *Women.* Evidently he was having far more success in that area than I was, judging from the scorching females that kept glancing his way, or strolling over and introducing themselves. *This* was a guy I knew I'd have to start hanging with.

So he started showing me around the Sin City nightlife scene. As a writer, I've hung around celebrities and known my share of "players," but when it came to interacting with women, Christopher was in a league of his own. Whether we were walking around the mall or hanging out at a bar, he could approach any woman that caught his eye, start up a conversation, and have her smiling and chatting in no time. From there, he could steer the encounter wherever he wanted it to go. Bear in mind these were what he called "hammers," gorgeous women who probably shoot down ten guys a day.

It amazed me how he managed to remain on great terms with many of his ex-girlfriends, thus providing him a huge pool of attractive female friends. It also meant that every time the two of us went out, there were hammers that wanted to accompany us and actually *help* us meet new women.

I'd never seen anyone establish bonds with women so quickly and effectively. He made it seem effortless—telepathic, even—as if he somehow knew exactly the right thing to say and do in every encounter. Then one day while we were chatting about our backgrounds, he mentioned that he was a former hostage negotiator. My ears perked up. When I pressed him for details, he told me about his extensive training and the many dangerous situations he had to defuse in the line of duty. He told me about the importance of "building a bridge" with hostage takers, and the techniques that negotiators use to gain their trust and deal with their demands.

Now it was starting to make sense. This *had* to explain his way with women. And the more he told me about hostage negotiations, the clearer this parallel became.

I immediately realized this was information that any guy could use, regardless of his age or background. So over the next year, I worked with Christopher to develop a system based around his training and experience: one that guys like myself could learn and put into practice. By day, we started putting ideas down on paper and fleshing out new concepts. By night, the Las Vegas party scene provided the ultimate testing ground. In the process, we spoke with countless women and men about their experiences with the opposite sex and uncovered a wealth of information. From all of this, one powerful theme emerged: what women are looking for, and what men *think* women are looking for, are often two very different things.

This book will teach you that women are not the great mystery most men think they are. Each has desires and needs that you can learn to identify and use to connect with them. Each has standards by which they judge men. And even the most stunning beauties have insecurities you would never suspect. If you can learn how to read and interact with them on a deeper level, you can crack the code to their hearts. You can then date them on your terms, instead of feeling the need to impress them or make them your girlfriend before some other guy comes along.

From the beginning of this project, Christopher stressed two points. First, *M.A.C.K. Tactics* goes much deeper than learning how to succeed with women; it's about discovering and developing the Mack that resides in all of us. Second, confidence isn't something you're either born with or not. It's like a muscle that can be developed and strengthened, as long as it's properly trained. *M.A.C.K. Tactics,* stripped down to its core, is about learning how to look inside of yourself, recognize your strengths, and transform yourself into the confident, empowered, unique individual that you are capable of being. That you *deserve* to be.

From personal experience, this is very powerful stuff, truly like nothing else out there. Once you've learned the strategies and techniques within this book, it's up to you how you're going to use them. If you want to soak up the singles scene and date a variety of different women, you'll be able to do that. If your goal is to find the woman of your dreams to settle down with, you'll have the confidence and knowledge to identify her and build a relationship with her. You'll also find that these abilities carry over into all aspects of your life, from dealing with friends and family to getting ahead in your professional career.

The lessons in this book are universal, whether you're a hipster on the nightclub scene or a middle-aged guy back in the dating game after a divorce. If you're shy around women, *M.A.C.K. Tactics* will help you break through those barriers. If you have a natural way with the ladies, the knowledge in these pages is going to elevate your game to a whole new level. If you're already in a relationship, it will teach you to communicate more effectively with your mate and make sure that *your* needs are respected and fulfilled. And we encourage all women to read this book. This way, you'll know when you're in the hands of a skilled Mack, or dealing with an amateur. You'll understand what confident men look for in women, and what the "red flags" are that cause men to lose interest. And believe us, the greatest favor a woman can do for a male friend is to teach him some tactics.

Joining forces with Christopher Curtis to create *M.A.C.K. Tactics* has been an amazing journey. Now it's time for you to climb onboard and take the ride for yourself.

Rob Wiser
Las Vegas, 2004

A Word from Christopher Curtis

Two years ago I would have laughed if you'd told me I was going to be the coauthor of a book about succeeding with women. When I first met Rob, I was all about going out and having a good time. It was my way of unwinding after the stresses of police work. I had a lot of great times with a lot of different girls, but I never thought what I was doing was anything extraordinary.

Ironically, it took another guy to make me realize that I related to women, and women related to me, on a higher level than normal. I remember sitting around with Rob while he picked my brain about different dating topics. I was actually surprised at how my answers flowed like water. For any question he asked me, I was able to lay out rules and strategies that I'd figured out over the years. He was impressed with the amount of information I had stored in my brain, but he still wondered how a guy like me could make it happen the way I did.

He started asking me about my background, and that's when I mentioned my former work as a hostage negotiator. It was just a passing comment that I thought he would think was cool. Then I saw his eyes light up. He'd figured out a connection that I wasn't even consciously aware of: when I interacted with women, I was taking the strategy and psychology that I'd learned on the job and putting it to work in a different way.

When he explained this connection to me, it actually made sense. So I started giving Rob some tips. We joked around that he was now my "Mack in Training." He began to apply the principles, and in no time he was having success with women way beyond what he was used to. I could also tell it was making him a more confident, outgoing guy. It made me happy to see the transformation. I started doing the same for my other friends, girls included, and before I knew it my phone became the hotline for advice (to the point where I had to change my number!).

Eventually, Rob and I went in the lab and created the book you now hold in your hands. Our goal was to create the ultimate product of its kind, and I believe we've accomplished that. I've checked the other dating books and Web sites. Some of them contain bits of interesting information, but trying to apply their lessons in real life is like learning just enough karate to get your butt kicked. These books fail to take into account that no two men are born alike. The opening lines and fashion tips that work for one guy aren't necessarily going to work for the next guy. You can give any house a fancy paint job, but what is it worth if it lacks a solid foundation?

This book is heart, soul, and science. It involves an inner growth that crosses over into all areas of your life. The lessons in this book will be of interest to women as well, because despite our differences, men and women share many of the same desires and challenges.

You are about to embark on one of the most fulfilling trips of your life. So, enjoy, grow, and have fun with this. Trust the process, put it to work, and become the Mack you were born to be.

What Is
M.A.C.K. Tactics?

Picture a house at the end of a dead-end street. A police helicopter hovers overhead, bathing the scene in a spotlight. An army of cops are massed on the perimeter. A heavily armed SWAT team has their guns trained on the house, waiting for the command to unleash hell.

A man is holed up inside, sweating bullets, clutching a gun. His ex-wife and kids are huddled in the corner. He screams his demands out the window: a taxi to the airport and a fueled-up plane going straight to Cuba. If these demands aren't met, there's going to be bloodshed.

Then a car rolls up to the scene—not the requested taxi, but an unmarked sedan. Out steps a man. Though average in size, he radiates an aura of total control and confidence. He coolly walks around to the back of his car, pops the trunk, and dons a bulletproof vest. From his calm expression, you'd think this is just another day at the office.

For this highly skilled hostage negotiator, it is. He has seen and conquered this situation a hundred times before. The circumstances vary, but the rules of the game are always the same. And this is a game he has mastered.

The negotiator begins to converse with the hostage taker

for the release of the hostages, and eventually for his peaceful surrender. It might take hours, even days, but the negotiator's focus and discipline never waver. Everything he says, every phrase he uses, is part of a strategy to build a bridge of trust. For everything the hostage taker says, and every demand he makes, the negotiator has a response that steers the encounter in the direction he wants it to go. He can already envision how this situation is going to end; now, it's simply a matter of guiding it there. Like a world-class chess player, he's always thinking several moves ahead.

The negotiator is confident, highly trained, and commands respect from his fellow man. He is a force to be reckoned with—on and off the job.

In other words, you might say he's a Mack.

Creating the System

This parallel, between hostage negotiation and the science of succeeding with women, is what spawned *M.A.C.K. Tactics*. Christopher Curtis comes from a law enforcement background and served as an actual hostage negotiator. He was the guy they called in when some maniac had taken his wife and kids hostage and was waving a gun around making demands, or when some sad soul had given up on life and was ready to end it all.

Time after time, Christopher was able to "talk down" these troubled individuals. He succeeded by applying specific principles and psychological techniques he'd learned through his training, and many hours spent in the field dealing with these situations.

He operated from a playbook that he had drilled into his brain. For anything the hostage taker said or did, Christopher was ready with the correct response. He was patient and disciplined. He kept his cool, formed a bond of trust with the hostage taker, and negotiated until the situation was defused.

But the work was physically and emotionally grueling. When his shift would end, he would often hit a nightclub or a bar to unwind and decompress. Living in Las Vegas, there was never any shortage of options.

Something interesting began to happen during these late-night excursions. When he met women at the clubs and bars, instead of engaging them in the usual small talk, he would subconsciously slip into "negotiator" mode—drawing upon his training and using those same principles and techniques in his conversations. He would deal with women in the way that would be most effective in a hostage scenario. Instead of talking about himself, he would listen and earn their trust. Instead of giving them reasons to say no, he gave them reasons to say yes.

His success rate boosted his confidence. Soon, he was throwing caution to the wind and approaching gorgeous women who had once intimidated him. It didn't matter how guarded they normally were toward men; once he started applying his strategy, the walls came down. Meeting new women every day became an adventure to look forward to, instead of being frustrating and stressful, as it was for many of his friends.

Christopher also began to discover parallels between hostage takers and the typical single woman. Both were jaded by past negative experiences and tended to be non-trusting. With women, this attitude was often a result of the way they had been treated by men, whether it was their father or an ex-boyfriend. But by establishing a bond with them, and gaining their confidence, Christopher was able to knock down those barriers and connect with them on an intimate level. In the process, he formed a belief that just as no encounter with a woman is arbitrary, every encounter with a woman must be viewed as a negotiation—the difference being instead of coaxing them off rooftops, he was coaxing them into romance.

The M.A.C.K. Tactics system was derived from these core strategies and principles. It's time to shed the doubts, anxiety, and all the other self-imposed handicaps that have held you back from achieving your full potential. Stop living in mediocrity and start living as a Mack.

Defining the Mack

Before we go further, it's important that we state our definition of a Mack. To some, the word conjures up images of a slick pimp in a fur coat and wide-brimmed hat, using his silver-tongued rap to get women to do his bidding. To others, the word suggests a sleazy pickup artist, forever on the prowl for his next conquest.

We define the modern Mack as a far more impressive and powerful individual. He is a man who possesses confidence, charisma, and style. He has a keen understanding of women: what makes them tick and what they truly want from men—not what society and the media have led us to believe they want. The Mack knows how to engage and stimulate women, mentally and physically, and establish a connection with them through words and body language. The Mack doesn't need to use lies or deception. Confidence, knowledge, and a strong mind-set are his greatest assets.

More importantly, the Mack has knowledge of self. He's in tune with his own strengths and vulnerabilities. He knows his strong qualities and how to highlight and capitalize on them. Conversely, he's aware of the areas that can be improved, and works on bettering his game on a daily basis. And while even the most gifted Mack gets rejected on occasion, he never lets it faze him. Blows that would crush an average man's confidence simply ricochet off the Mack's armor. In fact, they make him stronger, since every encounter with a female yields valuable lessons.

While the Mack's abilities make him intriguing to women, he uses these skills to great effect with men as well. The Mack understands that life is a never-ending series of negotiations, whether you're purchasing a car, asking for a raise, or dealing with a difficult coworker or family member. While routine daily challenges result in stress, frustration, and depression for the average man, the Mack's attitude and interpersonal skills enable him to navigate these obstacles and achieve the desired results.

For the Mack, there are no such things as problems. There are only challenges, which he enjoys tackling.

Also be aware that Mack status doesn't necessarily mean you're young, buff, or born with traditionally handsome looks. Donald Trump? Mack. Bill Clinton? Ultra-mack. Tony Soprano? Without question, a Mack—not a traditionally handsome guy, but you'd be surprised how many women find his hypermasculine onscreen persona incredibly sexy. Even without the wealth and fame, guys like these would be highly successful with women. We'll show you how to incorporate some of their winning qualities into your game.

Playing to Win

Though the primary purpose of this book is to teach you how to succeed with the opposite sex, mastering M.A.C.K. Tactics can start you on a path to success in all areas of life. Getting ahead in business has a lot to do with relationships—how well you connect with people, and how much they respect you. Which man is more likely to thrive in his career: the one who is desperate, willing to settle for any girl who responds to him, or the one who is able to charm and establish a connection with every woman who crosses his path? Chances are, the man who can achieve success with highly desirable women has the confidence necessary to negotiate his way to a promotion, a raise, or the best possible deal when buying a car or a home.

If you're taking the time to read this book, you've already demonstrated that you're ready. Now it's time for us hold up our end of the bargain. If you commit to this journey and begin applying these lessons in your daily life, the M.A.C.K. Tactics system is going to take your game to a level you never dreamed possible.

Desperate Times, Drastic Measures

We are a society of men raised by women.
—*Brad Pitt*, Fight Club

The situation has reached a crisis point for the modern man. Let's be brutally honest: the male species is weaker and softer than ever, and it's only getting worse. If you want proof of this trend, just check out an episode of *Queer Eye for the Straight Guy*, which was the hottest thing on television back when it first aired. It's got some clever little tips, and the "Fab Five" do know how to deck out an apartment. It's the underlying message that we find troubling: that the average man is so pathetic, so clueless, so completely lost that without the "feminine touch" he is doomed to a life of loneliness.

We're getting bombarded with this type of propaganda from all directions. Consumer culture tells the modern man how he needs to dress, what he needs to own, and how he's supposed to act in order to be desirable to women. We base our self-worth on the job we work and the car we drive. We're taught to follow the script and play by society's rules, in the belief that if we do so, we'll ultimately march down the aisle and settle down with a wife—not always the "woman of our dreams," but someone who placates our loneliness and saves us from the frustration and rejection we face on the singles scene.

Most men follow this script because they're afraid to go after what they truly desire. They play around on the singles scene for a while, suffer too much rejection or figure it's time to "get serious" with their life, then cash in their chips and settle down. Sometimes it's to the first female who's willing to give them sex on a regular basis. Of course they'd like to be involved with a beautiful, dynamic woman (maybe more than one at a time), the kind that cause other men to stare in envy. But these men have created rationalizations and excuses for their inability to land a dream girl. They invent excuses: that beautiful women are all gold diggers or that they're interested in "bad boys" instead of nice guys.

Make no mistake: gold diggers, consumers, and other types of negative women are certainly out there. *M.A.C.K. Tactics* shows you how to identify these categories of females so that you don't waste your time only to be hurt later. You'll also learn effective ways to identify the ones that *are* worth your efforts, whether your goal is to take home the hottest girl at the nightclub every Saturday night or to form a romantic relationship with a woman you've long admired. Whatever your circumstances may be, with *M.A.C.K. Tactics* you're no longer going to wait on the sidelines for opportunity to come knocking—because it probably never will. These tools will encourage you to get assertive and motivated.

Becoming successful with women is about much more than wearing the right clothes or using the right "lines." It starts by looking inward and creating a solid foundation. It means developing the correct mental attitude, changing the way you view women and yourself. Then *M.A.C.K. Tactics* works outward, helping you to revise your personal style and teaching techniques that will help you approach women, engage them in effective and interesting conversations, and build connections that distinguish you from every other guy who has ever come her way.

Start within, and build outward. That's the only way to make a powerful, lasting transformation.

Pillars of Power

Every one of the techniques and strategies contained in this book is for real. It's not about corny "pickup lines" or trying to fool women into believing you're something you're not. And it's not about the "numbers game" that your buddies at the bar might consider a viable strategy, hitting on a dozen women a night in the hopes that one will be receptive.

It is about mastering a system that is founded on a rock-solid foundation. The foundation of the average American male is shaky at best, and that is why *M.A.C.K. Tactics* is based on four powerful pillars: *M*ethod, *A*ction, *C*onfidence, and *K*nowledge. Applied correctly, they will support you through even the most turbulent circumstances.

Method. Pat Benatar said it best when she sang "Love Is a Battlefield." Before you deploy in the combat zone, you'd better have the right training and tools for the job. There is no universal strategy for macking women. Though all women share certain fundamental traits, each has different quirks that you need to be able to pick up on. *M.A.C.K. Tactics* teaches you how to recognize the different categories of females and how to employ the correct strategy. These strategies are often rooted in the same techniques employed by hostage negotiators. *M.A.C.K. Tactics* is the first system of its kind to incorporate this information.

Action. Nothing happens until you choose to take action. When it comes to women, more is lost by indecision than by bad decisions. But before you start making moves, it is imperative that you develop and hone the backbone of your personality. Which leads us to . . .

Confidence. This is the single greatest weapon you can possess in life, whether in the business world or in your personal relationships. The average guy views confidence as a trait that some were blessed with and others will never possess. This is false. Anyone can achieve self-confidence, and it doesn't require spending endless hours in the gym or making millions of dollars. What it does require is knowing yourself and learning to showcase your good qualities instead of burying them under insecurities and nervous habits.

We were all born with an amazing, even fool-hardy willingness to take risks. Remember how carefree you were as a little kid? You didn't think twice about climbing a tree. Our parents had to keep an eye on us, since we might jump into the deep end of the pool before we even knew how to swim. Nothing fazed us. If we fell down and skinned our knees, we might bawl for a minute, but then we jumped right back in the game.

Unfortunately, confidence and self-esteem are worn down with the passage of time. Failure, rejection, and disappointment have a cumulative effect. Some of us hold up pretty well over time, and exceptional individuals might even be strengthened by rejection—hey, it took Thomas Edison over six thousand tries to invent the lightbulb. But the sad truth is that most guys, by the time they reach adulthood, have been scarred by all the rejection they've had to endure. Rather than risk any further blows to their egos, they play it safe. This is why they wind up in relationships and careers that are unfulfilling.

Confidence is the number-one characteristic that women respond to. This doesn't mean swaggering around with your shoulders flexed;

that's usually the mark of an insecure man who's trying to cover up his deficiencies. Confidence means being comfortable in your own skin and maintaining the mind-set that you are in control of every encounter. Most women are willing to follow a confident man's lead. But you must take the lead.

Knowledge. When it comes to dealing with women, there are rules and principles to follow. And as complicated as they may seem, you can learn what makes them tick. With *M.A.C.K. Tactics* you will develop a thorough knowledge of female psychology. Equally as important, you will develop a strong knowledge of self. You need to understand the package you are presenting every time you introduce yourself: your strengths, your interests, and your attractive qualities.

Gathering intelligence (intel) is one of the cornerstones of knowledge. From the moment he notices an attractive woman, the Mack is registering details about her that will factor into his strategy. How is she dressed? Who is she with? What does her body language suggest about her personality—and her availability?

Once the conversation begins, the Mack says things to her that elicit further intel. He doesn't ask point-blank questions; instead, he uses subtle phrasing to prompt her to divulge details. Is she single? How long has it been since her last relationship? What are her favorite activities and types of food, in case this leads to a date? Are there any "red flags" he needs to be aware of? Is she in the market for a serious relationship, or is she looking to have fun tonight—no strings attached? It's all intel, and knowing how to acquire it makes you a stronger Mack.

Trust the System

A final note: in order to successfully learn the M.A.C.K. Tactics system, you need to place your trust in it. Some of the lessons in this book may contradict the way you've normally done things with women. Some of the approaches we teach may even be painful at first. For instance, when you meet a girl you like, your instinct might be to call her every day, try to take her on a fancy date, and state your feelings to her. As you will learn, this is a direct violation of Mack Commandment 1 (Flee and they will follow. Follow and they flee).

These methods have been proven to work, and the principles work hand-in-hand. If you ignore certain steps, others won't work correctly. It is the overall system that produces great results, not the individual rules and techniques.

Christopher Curtis tells a story to illustrate the importance of this system. When he entered the Marine Corps, he was one of the top recruits in his class but one of the weakest swimmers. (As a kid growing up in Queens, New York, the closest he ever got to swimming was splashing around in a busted fire hydrant.) He failed every swimming test miserably. He was embarrassed and frustrated, until one day an instructor coached him one on one. He showed Christopher exactly how he needed to use his arms and legs to swim effectively. Precise, powerful strokes, with all four limbs moving in sync. Over and over, he told Christopher to believe in the system.

At first, trying to swim that way, Christopher struggled and gasped for air. But he found that if he focused, and followed through with the strokes exactly as the instructor had shown him, he began to swim with speed and grace.

A lot of guys, when trying to interact with females, feel like they're drowning. Instead of using smooth, confident strokes, they struggle and flail. They look for things to cling to in social situations, such as drinking excessively or surrounding themselves with their buddies. When talking to women, they lie about their jobs and tell jokes instead of establishing real connections. After dozens, perhaps hundreds of failed encounters, they still can't figure out where they've been going wrong.

Let *M.A.C.K. Tactics* be your life preserver. Hold on tight, stick with the system, and you will start operating with power and confidence. You'll reach the other end of the pool in no time.

Fellas, it's time for us to take back the power. To put the Mack down. To put the four core principles to work: method, action, confidence, and knowledge. Your game will never be the same.

2

The Ten M.A.C.K. Commandments

The M.A.C.K. Tactics system is rooted in ten fundamental principles, which we call our commandments. Throughout the course of this book we're going to refer back to certain commandments, so take the time now to familiarize yourself with them. We'll start with number 10 and work our way down to the most important commandment of them all.

10. Success with Women Is Not a Mystery— It's a Science

We all know a guy, maybe a coworker or a friend, who has a way with the ladies. He's decent looking, but he's no George Clooney. He doesn't make more money than you do. And yet for some reason, women seem to find him irresistible. He's scoring left and right, while you can only wonder, "How does he do it?"

The good news is that it's not a mystery. It's not about luck, timing, pickup lines, or aphrodisiacs. Success with women is based on rules and principles that you can learn and master. And all women share certain needs and desires that you can learn to identify and capitalize on.

If you've been fairly successful with women, you've probably been following some of these rules instinctively without fully understanding *why* they work the way they do. Once you understand the science behind it, you'll be able to communicate with women on a far more effective level.

It's time for *you* to become the guy that makes your friends wonder, "How does he do it?"

9. The First Sixty Seconds Are Everything

First impressions are crucial in any encounter, whether you're on a blind date or interviewing for a job. Essentially, when you mack on a woman, you're interviewing for a position: that of her romantic companion. And where does a job interview begin? Not in the office, sitting across from your potential employer. It begins with personal preparation.

When you approach a woman for the first time, she pretty much decides within the first sixty seconds whether or not you are someone she'd be willing to have a romantic relationship with. She's sizing you up the second you make eye contact and judging you by certain criteria. While you're wondering what she would look like in a thong, she is trying to determine if you're possible boyfriend/husband material.

Are you safe to be with? Are you trustworthy? Are you the presentable, ambitious type—the kind of guy she can picture introducing to her friends or parents? Do you lead an interesting, exciting life—one that she can imagine herself becoming a part of? These questions and others are racing through the back of her brain.

Whether you're looking for a casual sexual encounter or

are in the market for a serious relationship, you always need to bring your A-game. Inside the space of that first minute, every aspect of your vibe—from the words you say to your body language to the way you interact with the people around you—needs to be on point. Once you've passed the "sixty-second test," you're going to use a succession of other tactics that we teach you in this book.

There's a saying that in every person's lifetime, they let at least one million-dollar opportunity pass them by. Be the exception to this rule by always being ready to capitalize.

8. Three-quarters of Macking Is Listening

When it comes to conversing with a girl, give a guy enough rope and he'll usually hang himself. During the initial conversation, you need to be direct and effective. Prompt her to open up about herself, but don't divulge too much information about yourself.

This first phase of the encounter should be considered a "recon mission." You're letting her talk and processing what she says through your mental computer: how recently she has been in a relationship, what kind of music she likes, where she works, which clubs she hangs out at, etc. We'll show you how to read this intel and use it to your advantage.

The more you say about yourself, the greater the chance that you'll slip up or say something you'll later regret. By listening, on the other hand, you will build a bridge of trust. The more she reveals, the more comfortable she will feel with you. You become her ally, just as the negotiator forms a bond with the hostage taker.

7. Eye Contact Leads to Body Contact

Eye contact is where it all begins, the move that opens the door and initiates the encounter. It's one of the surest ways to demonstrate confidence and establish a connection. The eyes are the window to the soul, and this form of contact can be as powerful as touch.

Just as eye contact is the first step, establishing body contact is a critical step that you will incorporate later in the encounter. *M.A.C.K. Tactics* will teach you ways to establish subtle body contact with her, breaking down the invisible barrier and enabling you to start connecting with her on a physical, romantic level.

6. Be Original

This is a huge commandment that covers a lot of ground. There are a lot of guys out there on the prowl who have no tact and nothing interesting to say. Any attractive woman could fill a book with all the lame pickup lines and cliché approaches she's gotten from men.

Whether it's the opening convo or a third date, you must always distinguish yourself from cliché guys, who we call the Wack Pack, and present yourself as a fresh, exciting alternative. Originality is important in every aspect of your Mack vibe—from the clothes you wear, to the way you make your approach, to where you take a girl to dinner. We're going to cover it all, from the fashion to the passion.

5. Tip and Tip Well

Compared to the other commandments, this one may sound rather minor. Trust us, it isn't. Tipping isn't about trying to look like a big shot. It's about showing the woman you're with that you're a generous person, and that you expect to be treated well and reward good service.

When your waitress brings the first round of drinks, tip her a few dollars more than you normally would. Rifle through the singles, hand them to her, and smile and thank her. Make it a habit to tip a bit more than usual when you're with female company. It's not about the amount of money. It's about the gesture, doing it so that the recipient of your tip, and the woman you're with, both take notice.

Cheapskates squirm while trying to calculate the bill and figure out whether to tip four or five bucks. What's a few dollars in the grand scheme of things?

4. Guide the Conversation

Guiding the conversation does not mean dominating the conversation. (Remember commandment 8: Three-quarters of macking is listening.) It means steering it in a subtle, "invisible" way so that you stay on topics that highlight your strengths and selling points, and away from your weak areas. At the same time, you elevate the conversation above the generic small talk by using a technique we call "creative phrasing." We'll cover this in depth in chapter 5, "Conversation Control."

3. Every Interaction with a Female Is an Opportunity

Being a Mack doesn't mean you only step to the hottest females you come across. It means you've got a Mack mentality 24/7, and you impress every female—regardless of their
looks or age—with your personality and courtesy. Every time
you encounter a female, whether it's a bank teller or a strip-
per, it's a chance for you to test your game and learn new
things about women. This is part of the concept we call "batting practice," which you will be hearing more about.

2. Wherever You're At Is the Place to Be

When a Mack goes out to have a good time, people notice
him. Whether he's at a restaurant or hanging at a bar, he and
his friends are obviously having a good time and sending out
positive energy. His table is the one everyone else wishes
they were at. He usually has at least one attractive female
friend accompanying him when he goes out macking, since
this boosts the overall energy level and makes the other
women in the room more curious to meet him.

You will sometimes find yourself in a wack environment;
maybe it's overcrowded, or the DJ is playing music you don't
like. But the Mack can always flip a negative situation into a
positive. When everything is going right—great music, room
to maneuver, lots of pretty women—anyone can have a good
time. The Mack knows how to adapt and send out positive
energy regardless of the environment.

1. Flee and They Will Follow— Follow and They Will Flee

This is the big one. Numero Uno. The summation of every M.A.C.K. Tactic in the system. Why? Because, typically, women want what they can't have. A lot of men are under the impression that the more attentive they are to a woman and the harder they pursue her, the better their chances of scoring are. They figure that by going above and beyond the call of duty, they will eventually win the girl over.

This might work in Hollywood romantic comedies; the nerd can get the cheerleader in the end by being persistent and professing his feelings to her. But in reality, this isn't the case. Confess your feelings to a woman, and you will usually become less desirable to her. Make yourself constantly available, and she'll begin to think you have no life outside of her. You must project the image of a busy guy, someone who leads a full, exciting life with or without her. You *won't* always be available to talk on the phone or meet up when she wants to. The harder you are to pin down, the more appreciative she'll be when you set aside time to spend with her.

Fleeing, so that they follow, isn't an easy principle to follow at first. Attention from an attractive female messes with the average guy's head. He thinks he needs to do whatever he can to seize the opportunity, before she slips through his fingers. But taking a more nonchalant approach is what will draw her to you. Make her think you're fitting her into your life, not the other way around.

Now that you're familiar with the commandments, let's show how you can incorporate them into your arsenal.

3

The Building of a Mack

*The most profound relationship
we'll ever have is the one with ourselves.*
—Shirley MacLaine

*A mind troubled by doubt cannot focus
on the course to victory.*
—Arthur Golden

Becoming a Mack is a process that will require you to make
some fundamental changes in the way you've been doing
things. More important, you're going to change a lot of the
notions you've developed about women—and about yourself.

The Renaissance Mack

Before you can start applying the strategies and techniques
of *M.A.C.K. Tactics,* it is essential that you understand the
man in the mirror. You need to aware of the kind of guy that
you are, because it's the package you present whenever you
approach a woman.

Being a Mack means distinguishing yourself from the millions of other guys out there. They may have better looks or bigger muscles, but those aren't qualities that women are necessarily seeking in a mate. When a woman sizes you up, she is imagining what a future with you would be like. Therefore it is important to present yourself as someone who is out there on the scene, who has interests and is enthusiastic about a variety of subjects. If you live life with a passion, she is more likely to develop passionate feelings toward you.

A Mack has developed a broad range of interests and is constantly gathering knowledge—not only about women, but about a wide array of subjects. Knowledge is gained through being inquisitive, and Macks are inquisitive people. They're curious about the world around them and are always learning. On any given day, they've got at least a dozen interesting subjects they can converse with a woman about. These don't need to be "deep" subjects like politics or relationships. They can be as simple as a new band he's been listening to, a great movie he saw, a cologne he purchased, a cool clothing store he checked out, or a unique restaurant he discovered. He projects the image of an enthusiastic, well-rounded guy who is out there *living* every day to the fullest.

Each Mack has his own areas of interest: cars, music, restaurants, travel, fitness, and movies are just a few. There's nothing wrong with being a sports nut or a comic-book fan, but realize that these are not subjects that most women want to discuss at length. Even if it turns out she shares your passion for the New York Yankees, you still don't want to stay on the subject for too long. It's important to demonstrate that you have a wide range of experiences to share. The fuller your life is, or appears to be, the more desirable you are.

Most men give the impression that they need a woman to complete them. The Mack already projects a complete image. He has his interests and passions. He's been on plenty of adventures, with many more to come. The message he sends to women is that he doesn't need a woman; rather, he's interested in women who he can share his exciting life *with*.

Identify Positives

One encouraging aspect of human nature is that we can easily identify the good qualities of others. If we asked you, you could probably tell us which of your friends have a great sense of humor, which ones have the best fashion sense, which are the most talented, which have a good head for business, and so on. You are keenly aware of the positive characteristics of the people close to you.

But when it comes to ourselves, most of us have a hard time identifying the positives. If someone were you ask you, "What are your three best qualities?" you might have a hard time answering truthfully. It's difficult to answer that question without sounding like you're boasting. Instead, most guys would rather deflect the question with a joke. This is because most guys have a hard time looking at themselves and honestly acknowledging their best qualities. Some guys have even convinced themselves that there's nothing extraordinary about them.

The result is that a lot of guys, every time they see a very attractive woman, have already subconsciously convinced themselves "I'm not good enough for her," or "she's out of my league." These guys assume that beautiful women require certain things that they don't have to offer, and that approaching her would be futile.

Sure, six-pack abs and a fat bank account give you a tactical advantage, but there are many other qualities that beautiful women are attracted to. Women are programmed differently than men are. On a biological level, they're seeking a mate, a father to their children, a man who can provide comfort and security. You have traits within yourself that cater to these needs, and these qualities are of much greater significance than bulging biceps or a Benz in the garage.

What you need to do right now, as a Mack-in-training, is identify the positives within yourself. Once you have recognized them, you can develop them and begin capitalizing.

This means taking "self-inventory." You are going to conduct an honest examination of yourself in order to identify your own strengths and interests. Imagine a new coach being brought in to run an NFL team. Before he starts cutting players, signing free agents, and whipping his team into shape, he needs to go through the roster, player by player, and see what he's working with.

In this situation, you are your own coach. You're going to examine your own locker room, see what kind of talent you've got, and start building a winning franchise.

Self Inventory

Pick up a pen and a pad of paper. Now you're going to make a list of your five best qualities, starting with the one that you feel is most important. No one else is going to see this list, so tell it the way you truly see it. (And yes, you need to actually *write these down*. This makes the exercise much more effective.) Are you honest? Trustworthy? Funny? Well-traveled? Do you stay in good shape?

Next, you're going to jot down ten things that you've done in the past year that you would consider positive. These "positives" can range from minor to major. We'll help you get started: the fact that you're reading this book says several very positive things about you. One is that you have a sincere desire to improve yourself.

Another is that you have a survivor mentality, because whether you're a teenager or middle-aged, never forget this: a lot of guys have already folded their cards and decided that they're hopeless with women. Rejection, failure, and low self-esteem have knocked them out of the race. But not you.

Mark your positives down and don't be afraid to give yourself props. Maybe you've got artistic or musical talent. Maybe you're good at your job. Maybe you're quick with a joke, or ambitious, or you're a loyal friend. All positives. Write 'em down!

Favorites

The next step in taking self inventory is to create your personal list of favorites. Having favorites defines you as an intelligent, opinionated person who knows what you like and is interested in the world around you. You're soaking up life instead of letting it pass you by. Favorites are extremely important when it comes to interacting with women, because a guy who can't discuss his own favorites is one who is wishy-washy, who seems like he has no idea what he wants. This is a huge turnoff to women. They appreciate a man who is decisive, passionate, and has opinions. We all have our favorites; some of us just have difficulty articulating them.

When macking, knowing your favorites is a great tool for carrying on conversations. It means you'll never get trapped in a "dead zone," an awkward silence where you don't know what to talk about next. When you know your favorites, there will always be subjects that you can bring up and discuss with her.

So now let's create your personal list. What is your favorite:

- **Type of music**
- **Musical artist**
- **Book**
- **Writer**
- **Movie**
- **Television show**
- **Actor and actress**
- **Sports team**
- **Place to go on vacation**
- **City**
- **Car**
- **Type of food**
- **Restaurant**
- **Beverage (alcoholic, if you drink)**

Let's look at an example. You're chatting with a girl and the subject of music comes up. She asks you what kind of music you're into. To this, the wishy-washy guy might reply, "I don't know—I like all kinds."

Nonsense. No one likes "all kinds" of music. He likes country music, gospel, and gangsta rap in equal measure? Highly doubtful. When a guy gives an answer like this, it's probably because he's trying to cover his bases. Instead of expressing a true opinion, he's trying not to contradict what the girl's favorites might be. This is the wrong approach to take in macking, and it's a lousy attitude in life as well.

Know your favorites and be prepared to explain why. There are no wrong answers; these answers define who you are as a person.

Quality Time

It's an expression you often hear in regard to relationships. Girls complain about not spending enough of it with their boyfriends; guys wish they could have more of it with the women they desire. But here's a news flash, fellas: the most important quality time a Mack can spend is with himself.

When he's on his own, the Mack is constantly exploring new subjects and expanding his knowledge of subjects that are of interest to women. This is a way of life that you must incorporate into your daily routine.

All women appreciate music on some level; we're sure you do, too, but your perspective may be limited. The next time you're at a record store, take some time to browse through the new music releases. Listen to some new CDs at the listening station. Maybe none of them spark your interest, but at least you're aware of what's out there and being listened to. You may not like rap music, but you should at least have a basic knowledge of who the top-selling rap artists are. The next beautiful woman you meet might be passionate about that music. You might be a classic rock fan, but you "date" yourself if you have no idea about the biggest rock bands of today. This knowledge can be gained in minutes by browsing music magazines and record stores the next time you're at the mall.

If you're at a bookstore, spend a few minutes checking out the new bestsellers. A great Mack question is, "What book are you reading right now?" or "What's the last great book you read?" You're showing that you're literate and that you value intelligence and knowledge. Attractive women find these types of questions refreshing, since most men focus on their looks, not their minds.

If you're interested in your appearance—and as a Mack, you need to be—visit some trendy clothing stores next time you're at the mall. You don't need to drop a bundle on clothes or start sporting a totally new look. (We'll give specific advice on this subject in chapter 4.) But start learning about the hot new brands, the looks that are in right now for both men and women. Use the salespeople as a resource for information.

The next time a girl asks you how you spent your day, you're not going to say, "I ran some errands." You're going to be specific and mention a cool store you checked out. You might describe a pair of jeans you were thinking about buying, or ask what she thinks of a new style that's all the rage with women right now. You might say that you visited a bookstore and were checking out an interesting title. Tell her about it and ask her thoughts on the subject. These are more than great conversational topics; you're also demonstrating that you're out there on the scene, keeping tabs on what's hot.

While you're at it, check out new colognes. You know those salesgirls that are always standing around behind the display counter, giving their cutest smiles and waiting to help customers? Now you've got a reason to interact with them. Ask them what the popular new fragrances are for guys; you can explain that you're shopping for a gift for your brother or father. Then ask them about the popular new fragrances for women.

Start being more inquisitive and aware of the world around you, especially when it comes to areas that women find interesting. Skim the weekly newspapers in your town that list special events, concerts, and parties. Start reading at least one news magazine (i.e., *Time, Newsweek*) on a regular basis. You're probably too busy to keep tabs on every new fashion trend, chart-topping singer, local nightclub, and political development. Even if you're not particularly interested in those areas, you should have at least a general knowledge of them. Come off like a guy who knows things, instead of relying on others to fill you in.

Another area to be aware of are current health trends. Subscribing to a fitness or men's health magazine is a solid start. By being able to talk about a new vitamin or dietary supplement you've heard about, or an exercise trend, you're conveying to the woman that you're interested in bettering yourself and that you're health-conscious. Women love men who take care of themselves. The underlying message is that you're an individual who's worth taking care of.

Make a routine of soaking up new information, and you'll

amass two things: knowledge and potential conversational topics. Be able to slip in a reference to that new fashion boutique, the cologne that just came out, or the best place to buy interesting jewelry or furniture. All of these little details improve your overall package. Being able to speak your mind on these topics paints you as an interesting, inquisitive, well-rounded guy—someone who is actively seeking out new experiences and trying new things, rather than depending on friends, magazines, and TV shows to tell him how to dress, where to go, and what to listen to.

A Mackin' State of Mind

Now, the next step. This one might make you chuckle at first, but trust us: it's a fundamental aspect of becoming a Mack.

You're going to create your personal mantra. Most successful Macks have at least one mantra that they go by. It could be a saying, a line from a movie, or even a song. Think of the unforgettable scene that opens the film *Saturday Night Fever*: John Travolta strutting down the street to the song "Stayin' Alive." It's one of the all-time great Mack moments in cinematic history.

From now on, whenever you're about to enter your Mack Zone, you're going to conjure up a song or phrase in your mind and let it be the mental sound track to your success.

Christopher likes to use the word "Unstoppable." When he walks into an environment where he knows he'll be interacting with women, that's the word that flashes through his brain—psyching him up, telling him that there is no obstacle that can get between him and his goal. When he walks into a party, he projects an aura: now that he's on the scene, the good times can *really* start.

Now we want you to make up one for yourself. Find one that suits your personal style. Here are some examples of mantras:

"The world is mine."
"Wherever I'm at is the place to be."
"Half man, half amazing."
"I can do this."

No one else needs to know your mantra. Consider these your personal code words, the ones that instantly put you in a macking state of mind.

Mack Fact: The amount of energy expended during sex is roughly equivalent to that required to climb two flights of stairs.

Batting Practice

In *M.A.C.K. Tactics,* we often refer to a term called "batting practice." The Mack is constantly taking batting practice, warming up so that when the right pitch comes along he's ready to hit the home run.

Batting practice means that you're constantly interacting with women on a daily basis, in a positive, self-affirming way. The girl who waits on you at the diner, your female coworkers, receptionists, bank tellers . . . with every female you encounter, even if it's an old lady at the grocery store, you're being charming, polite, and establishing a connection. Even if you're not romantically interested in her—and in many cases you won't be—you take the time to introduce yourself and say something to make her smile. By doing so, you distinguish yourself from every other guy she comes across.

The Mack makes a positive impression on every female he encounters. If a waitress serves a hundred customers in a day, the Mack is the one she will remember next time he comes in. He asked her name, took the time to chat with her about her day, and referred to her by name throughout their interaction. It's amazing what a positive impression you can make simply by introducing yourself, expressing interest in how her day has been going, and paying her a compliment.

There are many other benefits to adopting this mind-set. When you put forth positive energy you're going to get it in return. If you are charming and polite to a waitress, she is going to give you the best possible service. Take a moment to establish a connection with a pretty bartender, and she'll keep an eye out for when you need a refill. Car dealers, real-estate agents, sales clerks . . . just think about how many women you deal with during your day-to-day errands and activities. Imagine if every one of them had a pleasant opinion of you, remembered your name the next time you visited, and was willing to go the extra mile to help you out.

When you are constantly eliciting positive reactions from women, it boosts your ego and your confidence. At all times you are "warmed up," feeling good about your game, in a constant state of readiness. This way, when a hammer comes along, you are operating at your peak level. You've already had friendly interactions with a half-dozen women that day; now, instead of being anxious about talking to that girl who just walked into the room, you'll do what comes naturally. If you've been taking batting practice, your attitude will be more relaxed and confident. She'll pick up on this attitude, and it will distinguish you from all the aggressive, overanxious men she encounters.

By taking batting practice you are also constantly acquiring new knowledge about women. Strike up mini-conversations with the women you encounter every day, and you'll be surprised how much you learn about what interests them, as well as what bothers them. It's all valuable intel.

Mall Macking

Let's say you're out shopping for clothes, and a salesgirl asks if you need any help. The average guy didn't come to the store with the intention of meeting women, and figures the salesgirl probably has other things to attend to, so he tells her "no thanks" and keeps moving along.

The Mack move in this situation is to acknowledge her, give her a friendly smile, and say, "Right now I'm just browsing, but thanks." Then compliment her on a positive aspect of her appearance: "That's a really nice necklace you're wearing. Do you mind if I ask where you got it?"

It could be a pair of earrings, an outfit, or her shoes. It doesn't really matter; the idea is to isolate one aspect of her appearance and flatter her. She'll be more than happy to tell you where she bought her shoes or dress, which gives you a little piece of intel to file away. If it's an inexpensive but attractive necklace she bought at a local store, you now know where to buy one the next time you want to give a girl a gift. If she bought it during a vacation in Jamaica, it gives you a little gem to drop during a future encounter with a woman (i.e., "That's a nice necklace you're wearing. I was talking to this girl the other day, and she had this cool necklace that she bought in Jamaica. . . .")

You could just as easily have complimented the salesgirl on her hairstyle and said, "I really like your hair. I've got a female friend who's looking for a good hair salon." It will get the salesgirl talking, it yields more intel for you to file away, and if she's cute, guess what—the two of you are now having a conversation that could lead to any number of scenarios.

If you want to take the conversation further, ask her if the store has any cool new shirts or jeans for men. She'll be glad to show you the latest fashions, which is a great way for you to pick up tips. Be casual; this encounter is completely innocent and should be stress-free. It's not like you're trying to pick her up. Just remind yourself that you're only taking batting practice. If you want to get her phone number and see her again, you can always do that, too. (Later on, we'll show you the best way to make that happen.)

The effect of batting practice is cumulative. Make it a daily routine, and you will become so comfortable around women that talking to a woman for the first time becomes second nature. It's said that the best way to learn a foreign language is to live among the natives. If you are going to learn to understand women, the best way to do it is to constantly interact with them.

A player who only goes for home runs, like a guy who is only trying to hook up, is going to strike out a lot. His confidence will suffer and he will grow increasingly desperate. On the other hand, if you're constantly getting on base with singles, doubles, and triples, you'll be ready to swing for the fences when the right girl comes along.

Mack Visualization

After learning the lessons in this book, as you begin to apply the M.A.C.K. Tactics system with women and achieve victories, your confidence level will rise dramatically. Until then, we have some exercises that will help lay the groundwork. Begin working these into your daily routine.

After you take your morning shower, take a good long look in the mirror. Look into your eyes and take a few moments to get comfortable with the person that's being reflected back at you.

Call yourself by name and get comfortable with it. Your name is more than what people call you; it's the title you go by in this world, and it deserves respect. Reassure that person in the mirror that this will be another day of improvement, confidence-building, and successful macking.

Police officers use a concept called "positive self talk." When they're cruising the streets on patrol, they keep themselves sharp by running through mental scenarios. They envision dangerous situations and mentally walk themselves through them. When the real deal comes along, they're amped up and ready to take care of business.

A Mack is no different. When he's getting dressed for a night out, he's running through mental scenarios. He imagines situations in which he meets beautiful females and walks himself through the encounters step by step. He already knows the outcome is going to be successful. The mental exercise is about getting there, imagining the things he'll say and the moves he'll make to achieve that outcome.

Give this exercise a try: the next time you're standing in front of a mirror getting yourself together, imagine yourself in an environment where you often see beautiful girls. This could be your local mall, the beach, or your favorite bar.

Picture how you might begin a conversation with one of these hammers. If you're not the kind of guy who would normally walk up and start a conversation, *be* that guy in your mental scenario. Imagine her smiling at you as you approach. Then the conversation starts flowing. You're never lacking for something clever or interesting to say. She's enjoying chatting with you. Picture this encounter in your mind and walk through it, word for word, step by step. You're asking her questions, discussing subjects, and she finds every one of them interesting. As the moments pass, the connection between the two of you grows stronger. She can't take her eyes off of you.

Next, you're going to imagine the same encounter, but this time it goes wrong. Imagine yourself tripping and falling as you walk toward her, causing you to spill some of your drink on your shirt.

How would you recover from this? In real life, it might

cause you to abort the mission and turn back in embarrass-ment. But for the purpose of this exercise, you're going to imagine yourself making a smooth recovery. You pick up some napkins and brush your shirt off. You give her a smile, and she smiles back. You make your approach anyway, and the two of you have a chuckle over your little accident. She sees that you have a sense of humor about yourself. The ice has been broken; now, it's easy for you to introduce yourself and start a conversation.

Rehearse mental scenarios like these: the flawless intro-duction and the smooth recovery. Know that even if you say the wrong thing, or make an error, there is always a way to re-cover and maintain the flow. We call this Mack visualization.

Alfred Hitchcock, the legendary movie director, is a great example of the power of visualization. For many directors, shooting a movie is a very stressful experience. For Hitch-cock, who directed over sixty movies, being on set with his actors and crew was the most boring part of the filmmaking process. This is because he had already directed the entire movie in his head. He had created storyboards that mapped out every single camera shot and angle. The movie had al-ready been constructed in his mind, so that once the lights were set up and the cameras were ready to roll, the hard part was already over. It was simply a matter of executing—capturing his visualizations on film.

No movie, or conversation, ever goes exactly as you've "scripted" it. Actors may improvise; the director may sud-denly become inspired to try a new idea. In a conversation, the woman might go off on a tangent and the discussion will veer off into an unexpected direction. That's okay. This is what makes macking a thrill: the challenge of thinking on your feet, adapting, and still winning.

In baseball, you never know what type of pitch is about to come your way. But if you've been watching the pitcher and are confident in your swing, you'll be comfortable standing in the batter's box. You're ready for anything—the fastballs, the curveballs, and anything in between. You'd grow bored with the game if every pitch came straight down the middle. The thrill of the unknown is what keeps things interesting and forces you to keep improving your game.

Know Your Goals

When it comes to men, women are masters of recognizing "red flags." As they size us up, they notice the little things that we say and do—especially our mistakes. A single remark or a tacky shirt can cause some women to disqualify you.

The average guy, however, has few criteria when it comes to women. If she's good looking, he's willing to jump through hoops to pursue her. There could be red flags popping up left and right—things that would annoy him or lead to a breakup if this woman was his girlfriend—but as long as he's in "hunt" mode, he barely registers her negative aspects. She might be completely wrong for him, but at this stage he's like a race horse wearing blinders.

The Mack, on the other hand, knows what he's looking for and won't compromise. If he's looking for a one-night stand, minor personality defects might not matter. But if he's looking at women as potential dating partners, she must meet certain criteria. The Mack knows that the little things that irritate him now will cause major aggravation down the line.

If you want to date women who are self-sufficient, don't waste your time with one who is unemployed and lived off her last boyfriend. Maybe you hate smoking; you might be able to overlook her smoker's breath tonight, but won't it become a serious turnoff if you start dating her? It could be her body type, or the fact that she talks too much or has no sense of humor. Recognize *her* red flags and decide whether you're going to invest your time, or move on to the next one. And remember, there is always a next one.

There are women who have qualities that are outside your parameters but are still worth pursuing. Most people do have the ability to change. But for now, as you work toward becoming a Mack, it's important that you draw these lines in the sand and exercise self-discipline. This is not the time for compromise. This is when you should be building your confidence by choosing to rule out certain women, and only investing your time, energy, and money in ones that you can truly envision yourself being happy with.

Stand firm on what is acceptable to you, and what is not. This strengthens your ego and develops your confidence level. Instead of feeling like you are auditioning every time you approach a woman, adopt the opposite mind-set. She's auditioning for *you*. The ball is in your court. *You* are the one who is going to decide whether this relationship progresses to another level.

The Mack Pack

A soldier heading into combat must be properly equipped. Beyond the obvious essentials—helmet, gun, and boots— he's carrying with him an entire catalog of tools and devices that will sustain him through any number of situations, and perhaps even save his life.

Macks are no different. Experience has taught them that macking opportunities can pop up anytime, anywhere. That's why they never leave home without being equipped with a few certain items. We refer to this arsenal as the Mack Pack.

Lighter

Even if you don't smoke, you must carry a lighter with you at all times. You always want to be ready with a light if the girl you're macking needs one. This isn't just about being a gentleman. It's about being prepared to sustain the momentum.

If a girl you're conversing with takes out a cigarette and doesn't have a lighter, you're then obligated to go find one for her. In a crowded bar, this can turn into a wild goose chase in which you lose precious moments. While you're asking around for a light, the connection you've established with her is fading by the second. Meanwhile, the player sitting two seats down might be leaning in to supply her with one.

On a primal level, there's something masculine and reassuring about providing a woman with a light. Back in caveman times, the dude with the fire was the prehistoric equivalent of a Mack. Never be caught without it.

Breath Mints

You might think breath mints and chewing gum are one in the same. They are not. If you're a gum chewer you need to lose that habit. Chomping on a stick of gum doesn't make you look cool or nonchalant. It presents an air of cockiness, which some women find annoying. Most guys who are serial gum chewers are using it as a crutch (the same as cigarettes), whether they realize it or not; it gives them something to do, an excuse not to channel their full attention toward macking. If you want to distract a barking dog and calm him down, you give him a bone to work on. Gum has a similar effect on us. It dulls our edge and gives us something else to focus on.

Start packing breath mints instead. Besides keeping your breath fresh, a smooth by-product of mints is that when you pull them out of your pocket, by offering one to the girl you're demonstrating that you care about cleanliness and hygiene. Offering her a stick of gum looks tacky.

When conducting interviews with women during our research process, a common complaint they had about men was unpleasant breath. They encounter it from men all the time, yet none of us ever think that we're the ones that have it. Unfortunately, a lot of us do but are never aware of it, especially if we've been boozing. Our buddies don't tell us, because they don't notice.

The female "radar" is much more sensitive to this. They aren't going to come out and tell you your breath reeks, but once they detect it, you can forget about hooking up. It's a silent killer.

Breathing into your hand and then smelling it does *not* work. Don't take a chance on this. Carry a pack of breath mints and use them regularly—especially if you're drinking alcohol, and absolutely if you smoke cigarettes.

Cell Phone

In this day and age, the cell phone is a standard item for anyone. But you need to understand the deeper importance of
the cell phone. When you're trying to get her digits, you're
not going to do it with a piece of paper (or a cocktail napkin)
and pen. You're going to program it into your phone's memory. As we'll explain later, you can work this into a move that
is hard for a woman to say no to.

Make sure your battery is charged before you head out.
And if you've got some extra cash, invest in a nice phone.
The ones with built-in digital cameras make for a great conversation piece: take a woman's picture with a camera
phone, then look at the picture and smile as if you're amused
by the results. Naturally, being the vain (and self-conscious)
creature that she is, she'll immediately want to see how it
turned out. She'll scoot in close to check the picture, and
now you've got her in close proximity. It's an excellent technique for closing the physical gap between you.

Lip Balm

Besides your eyes and teeth, women will take notice of your
lips. A pair of moistened, fresh lips send a subliminal message to women that your mouth is approachable. Dry,
cracked lips are a big turnoff.

You should never offer to let a girl use your lip balm; she
may view this as unhygienic. But she may ask to borrow
yours, and if she does, it's a sign that's she comfortable with
you and considers you to be clean. But don't just hand it
over. Smile and preface it with a playful comment: "Just so

you know, I never let anyone use my lip balm—but for some reason I trust you."

Why the prefacing statement? Because you don't want her to think you'd let any stranger use this rather intimate product, just as you wouldn't let a stranger borrow your toothbrush. It also means that you consider her to be special.

As she uses the balm, check in with your inner Mack. How do you feel about her putting it on her lips? Is it sort of a turn-on, or are you slightly uneasy about sharing this product with her? This is a way to gauge how sexually interested you actually are in her. If you find yourself having reservations about her using your lip balm, you're probably not all that excited about the idea of kissing her. This means something about her just isn't clicking with you. If there are other female options in the vicinity, it may be time to bow out gracefully, move on to your next prospect, and toss that lip balm in the trash.

On the other hand, if you get a kick out of her running it across her lips, play it up. Make a playful comment like, "Now that you've used my lip balm, it's almost like we kissed." Notice how she reacts to this comment. If she laughs and seems intrigued by that notion, getting a kiss later on shouldn't be difficult.

Pen

If you've got a cell phone capable of storing digits, why bother bringing a pen? Because while macking, there are all sorts of instances when you might need to write something down. If you're conversing with a girl and she mentions a great book she's reading, or a party or concert that is coming up, you'll say, "That sounds really interesting . . . hold on a sec, I want to make sure I don't forget this." Then take out your pen, jot it down on something (perhaps a cocktail napkin), and put it in your pocket. It shows that you're sincerely interested and that you take her opinion seriously. You never know when she's going to give out some information that you need to jot down; maybe it's her home address, so you can pick her up for a date tomorrow night. How are you going to store that in your cell phone?

You never want to be put in the awkward position of having to hunt a pen down. Never assume that a waitress or bartender is going to loan you one; they're tired of drunkards borrowing their pens and never returning them. Have one on hand at all times.

Cash

Always make your entrance with enough cash for the mission at hand. If you're en route to a night spot, stop at an ATM on the way. Don't show up low on cash, figuring you'll find an ATM later. If you run out of cash in the middle of an encounter and have to go looking for an ATM, you might be giving another guy the opportunity to slide in next to your woman. Not to mention the fact that running out of cash raises red flags about your financial situation.

Paying with cash also makes it easier to discipline yourself. You're far less likely to buy women unnecessary drinks when you're dealing with a finite amount of cash in your wallet, as opposed to running a tab on your credit card (which also leaves you vulnerable to electronic glitches, and the possibility that your card could get declined).

On a side note, while conducting research for *M.A.C.K. Tactics,* we learned that when a lot of hammers go out to bars and clubs, they're not even expecting to pay for their own cocktails. They figure there will always be some guy eager to fork over money for their drinks; it's a form of power they like to exercise. Don't fall for it. It's about more than conserving your money; it's about maintaining the correct Mack mind-set. Reward them with a free drink because they look good and you've been enjoying their company. Never do it because you feel you're supposed to.

Condom

This one is obvious, but must be noted. Even if you're foolish enough to roll the dice on unprotected sex, don't assume for a second that she's going to go for it. If things are getting hot and heavy and she asks you about "protection," and you aren't packing any, it could stop the encounter dead in its tracks. If she allows you to go hunt down a condom, consider yourself lucky; you've implied that you don't normally take precautions about safe sex, and this sends a very sketchy message. Pack a jimmy hat and wrap it up.

The bottom line is this: when macking, you never want to find yourself in a position of need. The guy who has to scramble for a light, can't find a pen, or doesn't have enough cash for a tip looks inept. Women appreciate a man who never has to ask others for assistance. It shows that you've got your act together, a quality all women desire in a mate.

4

Mack Style: From the Fashion to the Passion

Macks come in all sizes, races, and colors. They come from all cities and backgrounds, from the cornfields of Nebraska to the urban jungles of New York. And just as there are countless types of Macks, there are countless types of Mack fashions—hip-hop, preppy, older professional, surfer, and punk rocker to name just a few. A guy with a mohawk who plays drums in a rock band can be as smooth with women as the buttoned-up corporate professional. It would look silly if either of these guys tried to adopt the other guy's style of dress, yet each can be a Mack in his own right.

No book or TV show can teach *you* exactly how you should dress. They don't know you, just as we have no idea what style would suit your body type, personality, or lifestyle. But we can help you assess your fashion sense so that you can take it up a notch. We can also point out certain fashion mistakes that no man should ever make.

Developing and enhancing your style is a learning process. Much of your learning will come from visiting stores, browsing, trying things on, and asking questions. We're not going to suggest too many specific brands, because they might not be right for you as an individual. Besides, new brands are always coming out, and we want to encourage you to constantly explore fashionable new options.

The fundamental message is this: *Your style should be the best possible reflection of who you are.* Every day, do you choose your clothes carefully and feel good when you're dressed right—or do you simply put on whatever clothes are comfortable or clean? If you fall into the latter category, it's time for you to start putting more care into your choices. This might mean taking some risks and experimenting, which a Mack should never be afraid to do.

First and foremost, having great style means you are *aware* of style. You keep up with trends, and notice when your fellow man—whether it's some dude on the street, or a celebrity on TV—is wearing something that might look good on you. We're not saying you need to start buying Armani, Versace, or the urban equivalent. But you *do* need to start pushing your own fashion envelope, especially if you haven't been successful with women. Feeling good about your appearance boosts your confidence, and as we've stated repeatedly, that's crucial to your success.

Christopher gets frequent compliments from men and women on the way he dresses. Ironically, the compliments often come from people who spend a lot of money on outfits and jewelry (we live in Vegas, where styles tend to be flashy), while he generally wears vintage (or "secondhand") clothing. He found a look that suits his personality: colorful, funky, a little bit adventurous. He could style himself in expensive designer brands, but he found a look that best reflects *him*.

If you were to try dressing the same way, you might feel uncomfortable and self-conscious. Then again, you might dig it—it does wonders for your self-confidence when you step out wearing something different and your friends (especially female friends) have a positive reaction. You won't know until you try out a couple of new "looks."

You must also remember that fashion is about more than knowing what to wear on a Friday or Saturday night. A lot of guys have several "special" outfits in their closet that they save for when they're going out on the town, but during the work week they pay little attention to what they wear. As a Mack, you should never leave the house without feeling good about what you have on. When you feel your best, your confidence level is high and you're better prepared to introduce yourself to whatever women you encounter.

Gyms are a perfect example: they're a magnet for attractive, in-shape women. Why enter a target-rich environment wearing old sweatpants and ratty tennis shoes? Invest in some hip workout gear, and the next time you go work out you'll feel sharper and more confident. You never know when a hammer is going to get on the treadmill next to you.

If you need to get updated on current fashions, browse upscale magazines such as *GQ*, *Esquire*, *Vanity Fair*, and *Men's Health* to see what hip guys your age are wearing. They may be wearing expensive designer threads that are beyond your budget, but it's the "look" you want to emulate, not the brand. There are probably stores at your local mall that offer moderately priced clothes in the same style. And as we've said before, saleswomen are always an excellent (and free) source of information.

While fashions change, there are basic rules you should follow:

No tight jeans. (Rule of thumb: if they show your "bulge" even remotely, get rid of them.) Ditto for acid-wash jeans, unless you're macking on chicks who still listen to Poison and Whitesnake. Restrictive clothing usually means a restricted attitude. As a Mack, you should feel loose, comfortable, and ready for anything.

Holster your "guns." If you hit the gym hard and have bulging muscles, we respect the effort. But don't show off your biceps with cut-off sleeves or shirts that are two sizes too small. We can already tell you're huge; walking around with flexed shoulders like you're "carrying luggage" only makes you look like a goon. Gratuitous displays of muscle are going to turn off more women than they're going to turn on. Better to save your physique as a surprise, once you get intimate with her.

Ditch the double denim. Don't try to match denim shirts or jackets with jeans. It looks like a missed putt every time.

No cheap shoes. When we say "cheap," we're not referring to the amount you paid. There are plenty of moderately priced brands, for both sneakers and dress shoes, that will look good with your outfit. Many hammers have told us that the first two items they notice on a man are his shoes and his wristwatch. If these two items are on point, they know they're dealing with a man who understands style. And don't forget the comfort factor; you spend more than half of your life on your feet, and if you wear cheap shoes you will pay the consequences.

Cool it with the jewelry. If you hang with the bad boy rock 'n' roll crowd, you can pull off an assortment of rings, chains, earrings, etc. But for most guys, here are the maximums: two rings, one on each hand. One necklace. One bracelet on one wrist and a wristwatch on the less dominant wrist. No more than two earrings. Even if it's good jewelry, when a guy wears too much it cheapens the effect. It's better to wear one nice item (a chain, bracelet, or watch) than several items that are imitation gold or diamond. Women know when they see the real thing. And if you wear a chain around your neck, tuck it in. Unless you're a rapper, guys with money don't need to advertise it with excessive "bling bling." **Rethink the baseball caps.** There are, of course, exceptions to this rule. If hip-hop is your style of dress, then a ball cap can definitely work with your outfit. But if you're a regular dude, don't wear baseball caps when you go out at night. Ninety-nine percent of women really don't care what your favorite team is. If you wear caps because you're going bald, think about shaving your head altogether.

Wardrobe Essentials

These are the fundamentals that every Mack's wardrobe should contain:

Three pairs of jeans. Every body type calls for a specific jean cut. Try some different brands and styles to see which fit you best. There are lots of cool options beyond the traditional blue jeans you wore growing up, in various styles and colors.
Two pairs of sweat/jogging pants. Blue and black are good basic colors.

One pullover sweatshirt.

Five button-down shirts. One should be a white dress shirt. At least one should be black, a color that always works when you go out at night. You should have three long sleeve and two short. Your most comfortable bet is to stick with 100 percent cotton.

Five vintage or vintage-style T-shirts. If you want to try a funkier look, check the vintage stores for T-shirts from the 1970s and '80s. Some have logos for old TV shows, movies, and bands. Since this look has now become fashionable, some stores sell new versions of these retro-looking shirts. They're a cool conversation piece and give your outfit a unique spin.

Two black T-shirts.

Two pairs of new-looking sneakers. One can be a pair of athletic sneakers, the type you would wear jogging. Your other pair should be a "fashionable" brand. Companies like Diesel, Steve Madden, and Sketchers make sneakers with trendy designs and colors that can be worn at night for a hip-but-casual look.

One pair of flip-flops.

One black suit.

One sport coat/blazer.

Two nice silk ties.

Two pairs of black dress shoes. *Always* wear dark socks with them.

As a rule of thumb, it's better to be overdressed than under-dressed. It's never a bad thing to be the best-dressed guy in the room, as long as you're comfortable and don't look strikingly out of place.

Dress Codes

Sometimes you'll be invited to an event that has a dress code. Here are some guidelines to follow:

"Casual" pretty much means anything goes. While shorts are okay, as a Mack you shouldn't settle for the bare minimum of what's acceptable. You're better off wearing a nice pair of jeans and either a collared shirt or a clean T-shirt. As far as footwear goes, no flip-flops and never any ratty shoes.

"Upscale casual" means wear a suit jacket, but you don't necessarily need to wear matching slacks. You can wear jeans or slacks of a different color. Wearing a tie is optional but preferred.

"Semi-formal" means a suit and dress shoes. You can opt to not wear a tie and keep your collar open, which can be a good look.

"Black tie optional" means some guests will be wearing tuxedos, but a dark suit is fine.

"Black tie" means a highly formal event where tuxedos are expected. If you don't own one, you'll need to rent one. Some guests will show up wearing suits, but they'll probably look underdressed.

In closing, any guy can look good in a thousand-dollar suit. The Mack is the one who can dress down and still look good—whether he's at the gym, chilling on the weekend, or at his job. That's having true fashion skills.

Mack Fact: Champagne was invented by a monk named Dom Pérignon.

5

Conversation Control

> *Wise men talk because they have something to say;*
> *fools, because they have to say something.*
> *—Plato*

There's a joke about two kids, a boy and girl, taking off their clothes so they can play a game of "doctor." The boy points to his equipment and teases her: "I have one of these and you don't." The girl points between her legs and replies, "I've got this, so I can get as many of those as I want."

This joke illustrates the basic mentality of most good-looking women. They know they've got what men want, and that men are willing to chase it. Attractive women are used to men bending over backward to please and impress them—and you can't blame them for it, because most men are eager and willing to go down that road.

Pickup Lines vs. Intros

Ask the average guy what's stopping him from approaching that cute girl across the room, and his answer will probably be, "I wouldn't know what to say." If he were to wind up conversing with her, he'd probably be fine; they'd find things to talk about. But it's that opening move, the icebreaker, that intimidates and paralyzes him from taking action.

There are a million bad pickup lines out there; most of them are so corny that they're not meant to be taken seriously. Some of the more clever ones might make her chuckle, but the conversation usually won't go much further than that. In her mind, when you use an obvious pickup line, you've just joined the pack of five hundred other guys who have tried to approach her and failed.

So, how do you make your opening move? The simplest way to "meet" her is to make eye contact with her from across the room and give her a smile. If you're having a drink, raise your glass to her and smile before taking a sip. If she smiles back, the door is open. This way, when you eventually approach her (or position yourself near her), you've already met in a sense. But wait to make that move. Don't make a beeline for her the moment she returns your eye contact and smile. The Mack is never in a hurry to work his magic.

Introduce Yourself

When it comes to starting the encounter, some so-called experts say you shouldn't tell her your name right off the bat. They claim that you should say hello, but wait until she tells you her name before you give up yours. If she does offer her name, their theory goes, you then know that she is genuinely interested in knowing you. Then you proceed from there.

This is a defeatist attitude; you're waiting for the go-ahead instead of taking command. Whenever a Mack steps up to a girl, he knows he is the one running the show. He never comes off cocky or arrogant, but is confident in the knowledge that he's the one dictating how the encounter will proceed.

Tell her your name right off the bat, look her in the eye and smile, and shake her hand. We call this the "three-point intro." This is the single greatest way to convey your self-confidence. Your name is who you are, and you are a person worth knowing.

"Hi, my name is Christopher. I noticed your outfit—
you look great tonight. I just wanted to tell you that."

The Name Game

From this point forward, remember that she is noticing everything you say and do. Some women, especially beautiful ones who get hit on constantly, are evaluating you from the moment you start talking. Other women aren't judging you consciously from the first moment, but make no mistake—their brains are registering every detail, determining whether you're "keeper" material or just another chump looking to score.

When a man doesn't offer his name right off the bat, it implies that he doesn't want her to know who he is. Maybe he's married or has a girlfriend and is trying to make something happen on the down low. Who knows; maybe he's wanted by the cops. The point is, on a subliminal level, holding back your name will only give her reason to generate negative suspicions. It's important to establish yourself as a trustworthy guy, someone she can feel comfortable with. So step right up, give her a smile and direct look in the eye, and tell her who you are. Think of this introduction as your verbal business card. Would you give a person a business card without your name on it?

As with most M.A.C.K. Tactics, there are deeper motivations behind this method. The Mack, always thinking like a chess player, likes to give his name up front because it also allows him to drop an effective line five minutes into the convo. The Mack will chat with her about this and that, and suddenly flash a playful smile and ask her, "What's my name again? Do you remember?"

The Mack says it playfully, like it's a pop quiz. It's an innocent-sounding question; if they're at a bar or club, it sounds like he's checking whether she's drunk. If she remembers his name (and usually she will, women are good with this), he knows the encounter is going as it should. If she doesn't remember, that's okay too, because it allows him to rib her about it, make her feel a little flash of guilt, and chalk up an IOU. (We're going to fully explain IOUs later on in the "Negotiations" chapter, but it basically means that you've caught her slipping up and called her on it. By doing so, you've planted the seed in her head that she "owes you one.")

When it comes to *her* name, remembering it is of paramount importance. Men are notorious for forgetting girls' names, and if you do so you've just dug yourself into a deep hole. One trick for remembering a girl's name is to repeat it out loud, slowly and with a smile, after she tells it to you. Say it like you really dig the way it sounds. Women love hearing their own name out loud. Make a Mack Mental Note (MMN) of her name and do not forget it. You're going to want to use her name in the conversation that follows.

If you do forget her name—and in a noisy environment, especially after a few drinks, it can happen—don't ask her to tell you again. That's going to make you look drunk or inattentive. The M.A.C.K. Tactics solution to this challenge is to create a reason for her to repeat her name without your having to ask directly.

Check out this Mack scenario. You've been talking to a girl at the bar for ten minutes, when you realize that you've forgotten her name. Some friends of yours are making their way toward you, and you know you're going to have to introduce the girl to them. You need to get her name to avoid looking stupid, but obviously you don't want to have to ask her again.

> *You* (looking across the bar at a random girl): "Wow, that girl over there looks just like my friend Jessica."
> *Her:* "Yeah?"
> *You:* "I was at her birthday the other day. I felt bad for her, they spelled her name wrong on the cake . . ."
> *Her:* "How'd they spell it?"
> *You:* "The normal way. But she spells hers differently: J-E-S-S-I-K-A. These days a lot of people spell their names differently, do you ever notice that? How do you spell yours?"

At this point, she'll either spell her name out or mention it in her response (i.e., "Lisa, just like it sounds"). This technique is money, because in this day and age, practically every female name—from Sarah/Sara to Catherine/Katherine—has a possible alternate spelling. Even if her name is totally basic, she'll repeat it in response to your question.

When she repeats her name, you're going to listen up, register the name in your brain with a solid MMN, and then it's back to the convo. Always remember: like a chess player, you've got to be thinking a few moves ahead. Any question you want the answer to, there is a way to obtain it without having to ask directly. The "name recovery" is a classic example. Instead of coming right out and asking her to state her name again, you invent a quick scenario that prompts her to divulge the information.

In some scenarios, you might opt to simply ask her to say her name again. If her name is "Kim," for instance, the above example might come off sounding a bit silly. In this case, be apologetic and sincere. Touch her arm and say, "I'm so sorry, could you tell me your name again?" There is no excuse for forgetting it a second time.

Her name is also important because you're going to use it throughout the conversation. ("So, Lisa, what do you think of this place?" or, "Which side of town do you live on, Lisa?") Psychologically, it makes a big difference if you occasionally refer to her by name. It reinforces that the two of you have a personal connection. You might be the only guy in the room that she has told her name to. This automatically distinguishes you from the Wack Pack.

Great Expectations

Another thing to keep in mind: if you're in a social environment such as a nightclub or bar and are feeling reluctant about approaching women, remember that the single women are there *expecting* to be approached. If they wanted to be left alone, they'd be chilling at home. They're dressed up, wearing makeup, and they want to be in the mix; it's just a matter of who they want to be in the mix *with*. She's waiting to be approached by a guy. That guy might as well be you. Again, the way to get the ball rolling is a confident, friendly approach.

Control, Don't Dominate

You can make more friends in two months by becoming interested in other people than you can in two years by trying to get other people interested in you.
—Dale Carnegie

So you made your intro, and now the two of you are chatting. This convo is how it all begins; the delicate dance in which the Mack presents himself in the best possible light, gets a read on the woman, and begins to guide the encounter.

The average guy will instead surrender control of the conversation. He figures as long as the woman keeps talking to him and smiling at his jokes, he must be doing something right. Meanwhile, the conversation is stuck in neutral when he could be shifting it into high gear and making sparks fly.

Other guys are too aggressive, talking too much or making sexually suggestive comments when it isn't appropriate to do so. The bottom line is that you must never take a conversation with an attractive female for granted. Use the proper strategy and you can control the encounter and the outcome.

Every conversation with a female is an opportunity for you to test your techniques and build a romantic connection. The key lies in knowing how to take the reigns and guide the conversation to where it needs to go. Learning conversation control is a key step.

But first, allow us to clarify one key point: when we say "control," we don't mean "dominate." You're not running your mouth, telling stories, trying to be the life of the party. You're never coming off aggressive or overbearing; these are signs of desperation. Your goal, as a Mack, is to guide the conversation without her knowing it. You will steer it in a direction that builds a bridge between you and her, creating a subliminal (and eventually a physical) bond.

Instead of wasting time with superficial small talk, every sentence out of the Mack's mouth has hidden intentions—whether it's to make her feel more comfortable, to gather intel about her, to draw attention to his own good qualities, or to strengthen the romantic connection.

The key lies in asking the right questions and touching on the right topics. You're going to encourage her to divulge information about herself and provide you with intel, which you'll use to your tactical advantage. Meanwhile, you will keep the conversation interesting, guiding it along with a gentle hand, creating a comfortable, entertaining scenario that sets you apart from the million other dudes on the scene.

Always keep Mack Commandment 8 in mind: "Three-quarters of macking is listening." When you assume the role of the listener instead of the aggressor, she reads you as a cool, nonchalant guy who's simply enjoying her company and doesn't have any expectations. You don't come off as anxious, a quality that is poisonous. Your vibe says, "I don't need her. I could be spending time with any girl in the room, but I'm going to give this one a chance because I like her style."

Mack Fact: Eighty-two percent of all marriage proposals are made by men.

Guiding Force

Look for ways to guide the conversation toward your positive qualities. You want to be able to mention them without lingering on them; the idea is to "plant seeds" rather than blab about yourself. Travel is an excellent topic to move the conversation toward. If you've seen some interesting parts of the world, talking about it makes you seem worldly, sophisticated, and adventurous—all qualities that women like. A man who travels is a man who can take her places.

To get on the subject of travel, simply wait for an opening, then slip in a sentence that references one of your travel experiences.

For example:

Her: "So do you like your job?"
You: "I do, but to be honest, I'm looking forward to

taking a vacation. I can't wait to get back to Europe. I had an amazing time over there."

It's as simple as that; you are now on the topic of Europe. You have guided the conversation away from jobs—a rather dull topic—to the exciting subject of international travel. You get to tell her about your experiences in an exciting, exotic destination. If it was ten years ago during your college semester abroad, or if you spent the whole time drinking and chasing women, omit those details. Talk about the interesting things you saw, the funny details you noticed about the culture, and describe what an amazing place it is. Spark her imagination. Paint the picture. Allow her to visualize it.

Keep it brief, hit the high points, and make it clear how much you love traveling and mention the places you plan to visit in the future. She'll be thinking about what it would be like to join you.

If you haven't visited any exciting foreign cities or countries, it simply means you need to do some Mack preparation before your next mission. Think of some places you'd love to visit someday, the more exotic the better. Research them on the Internet. Learn some facts.

The next time you're in mid-conversation with a female, you simply say, "I'm really looking forward to taking a vacation. I'm thinking about going to (insert country), I hear it's incredible."

The basic effect is the same. You're establishing that you're not like most guys; you're curious, worldly, and want to experience other places and cultures. Her brain registers this. You've placed yourself in a category above the average musclehead.

Creative Phrasing

The average guy feels awkward about approaching girls because he worries his opening lines will sound obvious and cliché. He doesn't have anything clever to say and knows he'll have to resort to something along the lines of "So, do you come here often?"

Once you've made your three-point intro, there's nothing wrong with starting the conversation with a simple question along those lines. The trick lies in how you phrase it. We refer to this concept as "creative phrasing." This means rewording the question so that it sounds fresh and original, and prompts her to give a thoughtful response.

If she's well dressed—this could be as simple as a nice-fitting pair of jeans—a great way to break the ice is to compliment her on her outfit. Attractive women take great care with their appearance. If you spent two hours at the mall shopping for the outfit you've got on, and spent an hour getting your hair just right, wouldn't you want to be noticed? Wouldn't it feel nice to have a stranger recognize the time and effort you put into how you look? There is no reason to feel shy about paying a girl an original compliment.

Be specific. If she's wearing an eye-catching skirt, blouse, or shoes, or has a stylish-looking purse, single out that aspect and compliment it. But *never* compliment her on how beautiful she is. That is a deadly cliché that attractive women hear on a daily basis from overaggressive guys. Tell her she has great style instead. No woman ever gets tired of hearing that.

When you deliver the compliment, it's important that you sound sincere. She needs to feel that you are genuinely impressed. She'll know if your words are empty and fake. If you sound honest, she can only be flattered.

Attach a question to the compliment, and you'll open the door to a conversation. "I just wanted to tell you that I noticed your outfit. I love that color. I'm just curious—where did you get that dress?"

If the girl is fashion-conscious, which is very likely the case, then it's a subject she enjoys talking about. Chances are she'll tell you where she bought it. If she wonders why you asked, tell her you need to shop for a birthday present for a friend, and thought that the item you noticed (purse, skirt, shoes, etc.) might be a good gift.

This compliment/question accomplishes a number of things. You're showing that you noticed a specific detail about her, while most guys only stare at her body; that you appreciate good style; and that you're a generous person who buys nice gifts for the people close to him. What woman would be turned off by those qualities?

Now that the door is open to a conversation, you're going to act casual and nonchalant. But remember, everything you say from this point forward is calculated. You are going to pose questions, give answers, and guide the conversation with an invisible hand.

If you are in a nightclub/bar, do not offer to buy her a drink at this stage. It may seem like the natural thing to do, but it's too soon for you to lay out cash. First, you need to get things flowing and also determine whether this girl, regardless of how beautiful she is, is worth your time and money. You are the Mack, and the Mack is the one in charge of the encounter. Adopt the mind-set that it is yours to continue, or cancel. You can always move on to the next.

Questions should be creatively phrased to avoid giving her the option of a simple "yes" or "no" answer. You want her to open up and talk, not respond with a single word. Relating this principle to law enforcement, there is a trick that cops use when they're trying to get a crook to spill the beans.

Let's say a cop suspects a guy of robbing a house on Main Street last night around midnight. The wrong way to phrase the question would be, "Were you on Main Street last night at midnight?" This allows the suspect to simply answer no and leave it at that. It is an easy question to dodge.

The more effective question is always, "Where were you last night at midnight?" Note the difference. Now the crook is forced to elaborate and come up with an explanation. He may hesitate (which indicates guilt), or he may be forced into a lie (which can be turned against him).

Not that you'll ever want to take an "interrogation" tone with women, but understand the difference between asking a yes/no question, and encouraging a more thoughtful response. Note the difference between the questions "Do you come here often?" and "So what are your favorite places to go out to on the weekend?"

Word Power

Negotiators constantly use creative phrasing with hostage takers. One example, which can be directly applied to macking, is how a negotiator will never use the word "gun." Instead of saying, "I need you to lower that gun," he'll say, "I need you to lower *that thing*." The mere mention of the word "gun" carries negative, violent connotations that might make the hostage taker more excitable. Calling it a "thing" diminishes the weapon's power.

Apply the same principle when a girl talks about her

boyfriend or ex-boyfriend. Never refer to him by his name; refer to him as "that guy," diminishing his significance. He is not an actual person to you, he is an abstract subject that isn't worth discussing (i.e., "It sounds like you had some problems with that guy, but I'd rather focus on you and me right now.") Attach zero importance to him, and you will encourage her to do the same.

Jobs

In the opening stage of the encounter, a standard question some women will ask is, "So what do you do?" (Especially if you're in a big city like New York or Los Angeles, where people tend to be career-oriented.)

As a Mack, you're not the average guy. This means you don't give standard answers to standard questions. You should always put an original spin on things and maintain a power position. Say with a playful smile, "I'll tell you what I do, since you asked, but if I answer then you have to answer one of my questions."

Then, answer her question succinctly by simply telling her what industry or field you work in. Do not launch into an explanation of what your job entails; this sounds self-centered and might bore her. If you have a lofty-sounding job title, such as executive vice president of something or other, don't bother mentioning it at this point. If she is genuinely interested in hearing specifics about your job or career, she will ask. This is when you can go into more detail.

If you have a job that is less than impressive, don't lie; just mention the general industry. The succinct answer lets you move off the topic and on to something else. This is a principle we call "articulate avoidance."

Whether you have a lucrative career or not, give the impression at first that it isn't terribly important to you. Portray yourself as confident but modest, like you're the type of guy who doesn't want women to be attracted to him because of his career or his bank account—just as women don't want men judging them solely on their looks.

From Wack to Mack

As you converse, use creative phrasing to put a spin on other cliché questions. A generic question when you're chatting with a girl would be, "So what kind of music do you like?"

In response to a generic question, she'll probably give a generic answer: "I don't know . . . I like all kinds of music." Lame question, lame answer, and you haven't made any progress. You're trying to fill dead space instead of moving things forward.

Instead, give the question an original spin. Smile and say to her, "Let me ask you a question. What CD is in your car stereo right now?" Or, "What station is your car radio set to right now?" If you're in a nightclub, the creatively phrased question might be, "What do you think of this DJ?"

The following are some other examples of weak questions (Wack Tactics), followed by a way to phrase them creatively (Mack Tactics). You will also see that creative questions can accomplish several goals at once. Just remember to always have your own answers ready to go.

Once she gives her answer to a question you ask, be prepared to give your own, and explain why. Never make an inquiry that you are not prepared to answer for yourself in an interesting way.

These questions tend to sound more natural if you preface them with the phrase "Let me ask you a question." Read them out loud. Test them out. Creatively phrased questions make you sound like an interesting, inquisitive guy who is sincerely interested in knowing more about her. They can make a conversation come alive and open gateways to all sorts of topics.

> **Wack Tactic:** "Who's your favorite actor?"
> **Mack Tactic:** "Are there any actors that you think are really sexy, but most people might not think they're attractive in the normal sense?" (This question can just as easily apply to music; just substitute the word "musicians" for "actors.")

Women will almost always have an answer for this one. The question usually cracks them up; they're a little bit embarrassed to admit the unconventionally handsome guy who gets their motor running.

In this scenario, not only have you posed a clever question, but by asking it and then giving your own personal pick you're establishing that you don't judge girls by the standard definitions of beauty. You have your own style and tastes. You recognize beauty where others might overlook it.

Just as importantly, when she shares her answer with you she's told you a little secret about herself. You know a quirky detail about her that no other guy in the room does. This automatically strengthens the bond between the two of you.

Wack Tactic: "Have you seen any good movies lately?"
Mack Tactic: "What's the most romantic movie you've ever seen?"

This is a question you might ask once an intimate mood has been set—on a dinner date, for instance, when the two of your are vibing and you want to shift her thoughts toward romance. This example of creative phrasing also establishes that you have a romantic side to your personality. Remember her answer. If you wind up having her over to your place for a "movie night," you know which DVD to have on hand.

Be prepared to not only name your favorite romantic movie, but to explain why you find it so romantic. Describe a memorable scene from the movie. Show her that it really made an impression on you.

Wack Tactic: "So what kind of food do you like?"
Mack Tactic: "What was the last really great restaurant you went to?"

This question opens the door for you to then talk about your own favorite restaurants. This is your opportunity to establish that you're a guy who appreciates good food and good service. If you like exotic cuisine, even better—it shows that you have broader horizons than the average guy.

Here's the bonus: once you know a restaurant that she loves, you can use it as a suggestion when you eventually take her on a date. (Assuming that it's not too expensive; we'll explain this in our "First Dates" chapter.) She'll be impressed that you remembered it. Most guys wouldn't.

Creatively phrased questions force her to think and respond in a genuine way. Effective conversation means connecting with her on a one-on-one level. You're getting to know things about her, and she's getting to know things about you—but only the things you want her to know.

Humor

Women say it all the time: a sense of humor is a very desirable quality in a man. This gives hope to a lot of guys who aren't traditionally handsome but are quick with words. The problem is that for most "funny" guys, their sense of humor is a defense mechanism. They're insecure about trying to connect with women, so they keep things light and try to make a joke out of everything. Don't think that just because you're making her laugh that you're building any real connection. The more she laughs, the less she is focusing on romantic possibilities.

There is also a big difference between humor and wit. Humor is a hand grenade; wit is a sniper rifle. You want to demonstrate the latter quality instead of being the guy busting out joke after joke, trying to be the life of the party. It's better to pick your moments to make witty comments and observations. And don't laugh out loud at your own lines; deliver them with a smile, and let the ladies do the laughing.

If you were born with a sharp sense of wit, you've got a great advantage with women. If not, the good news is that this is a skill that can be developed. The best way to do so is to listen and learn from your favorite comedians. Notice the topics they riff on and the way they deliver their punchlines. Usually, the more "straight" their delivery is, the funnier they are. As you build yourself as a Mack—and learn more about music, movies, books, and current events—you will be able to make more clever observations about things.

Save the constant one-liners and raunchy stories for when you're hanging with your buddies, and stay away from telling drawn-out jokes (i.e., "Three guys walk into a bar . . ."). Think about how awkward it feels when someone you don't know starts telling a long-winded joke. You're all standing around waiting for the punchline, and if it isn't funny you still need to chuckle out of politeness. Besides, the funniest jokes are usually the dirty or politically incorrect ones, which may alienate or offend her.

When you're around women, don't tell jokes at the expense of others. Don't crack jokes about any of your buddies; not only is that being a lousy wingman (as we'll explain in the "Wingmen" chapter), but it creates an awkward atmosphere. And if you've got a self-deprecating sense of humor, keep it in check. Your goal is to build yourself up in her eyes, not knock yourself down.

Just remember that while the occasional well-timed line can make you look sharp and clever, your primary focus should be listening, guiding the conversation, and strengthening the bridge.

Minimal Encouragers

Remember that as you converse, you're letting her do much of the talking. Resist the urge to jump in and start telling her what you think. Instead, use "minimal encouragers" to keep things flowing.

Some examples of minimal encouragers are:

"Wow. Listening to you talk, it seems like we're really on the same page. Tell me more."

"I was thinking exactly the same thing."

"I feel the same way. It seems like we definitely have some things in common."

"That's an interesting concept. Tell me how you came up with it."

"Is that right?"

"How did that make you feel?"

Women appreciate a man who listens. As she tells you about herself, and you acknowledge and appreciate what she's saying, it reinforces the bridge you're building between the two of you. The better a listener you are, the more comfortable she will become around you. Every time you agree with something she says, or tell her you feel the same way, you make her feel good and give her ego a little boost. This also spins the conversation so that she's trying to impress you with her thoughts and answers. Normally, it's the guy who is put in this position.

Mood Killers and Articulate Avoidance

There are certain topics that you should always avoid when talking to a female you're trying to mack. These topics include:

1. **Death**
2. **Communicable diseases**
3. **Violence/rape**
4. **Porn**

These sound obvious, we know. What kind of idiot would start discussing porn or rape with a girl he's just met? But there's a reason we mention these "mood killers," and that's because you can still fall into these conversational traps if you're not careful. If the woman happens to mention one of these subjects, some guys will then assume that it's okay to discuss.

It's not okay to get into an extended discussion on any of these topics, but you need to know how to deal with it if one comes up. If you try to change the subject too quickly, it will make you sound uptight, or even worse, like you have something to hide.

Here's the trick: if she touches on a topic that is a mood killer, you don't change the subject right away, but you don't linger on it either. You go into hostage negotiator mode. We'll explain in-depth how negotiations apply to macking in the next chapter, but for now, let us drop one example on you.

A common situation that negotiators face is the guy who's holed up inside a house with his woman, threatening to kill her (and himself) because he found out she's been cheating on him. The negotiator will identify and empathize with the hostage taker and become his "fellow traveler." He will explain how it would make him feel if he was put in that same type of situation. By doing so, the negotiator creates a bond between himself and the troubled individual. He understands his pain.

So let's say she brings up the fact that her best friend has an abusive boyfriend who beats up on her. This is a mood killer that you don't want to dwell on, but you don't want to sound dismissive either. The correct way to play it is to use articulate avoidance: "I think any type of violence against women is totally unacceptable. I think about something like that happening to my mother or my sister, and I don't think I could ever handle that." Then you segue to another topic.

The above example of articulate avoidance also accomplished a secondary goal. You mentioned your mother and implied how much she means to you. Women notice this; a man who treats his mother well is likely to treat her well. You don't want to overdo it—there's nothing sexy about a "mama's boy"—but the occasional mother reference will plant another seed in her brain, that you're a guy who respects and appreciates women. Conversely, if you complain about what a pain in the ass your mother is, that plants a negative seed. If a man can't appreciate his own mother, how can he appreciate a woman his own age?

Your goal as a Mack is to transport her into another reality—a "comfort zone" where the problems and evils of the world do not exist. You want to keep the focus on fun, exciting subjects that stimulate romantic possibilities.

Advanced Mack Maneuver: Polite Interruptions

Once you're in a groove and the conversation is flowing, inject a "polite interruption." While she's telling you a humorous story, give her a slight touch on her forearm—or if you're sitting next to her, on the leg—and pay her a quick compliment. It should feel spontaneous, but in reality it's a Mack Tactic.

"I'm really into what you're saying, but I just had to tell you—you have the cutest smile while you're telling this story. I'm sorry, go on."

If there's a good vibe between you, this should cause her to smile and perhaps blush. The trick is to say it like you couldn't help yourself; the look on her face was just too cute to resist commenting on. When she returns to telling her story, the chemistry between the two of you should be even stronger. That slight bit of body contact has just removed the invisible barrier between you. From this point forward you should be leaning in closer, narrowing the physical gap.

Later on we'll go into more detail about establishing body contact, but the polite interruption is an excellent method for establishing it early in the encounter.

Baiting Questions

Be careful about "baiting questions" that women may ask you. Never underestimate the female mind; they have crafty tactics of their own and might slip in an innocent-sounding question in an attempt to expose a chink in your armor. If you give the wrong answer, it is a pitfall that can extinguish any romantic interest she has in you.

A common baiting question women ask is, "How come you don't have a girlfriend?" This is never an innocent question. There's an intention behind it: she's trying to find out if you're a "player" who bounces from one woman to the next.

Answering in a cocky way is the wrong move. Don't say something like, "I like to play the field," or "I have plenty of girlfriends, I'm just not ready to settle down."

Instead, answer in a way that separates you from the herd. Tell her, "I'm not in a hurry. When the right girl comes along, I'll be ready." And this is the honest truth: as a Mack, you're not in a rush to make anything happen but are prepared to capitalize when opportunities arise. Now that you've answered her question, move to another topic. Don't let her start asking questions about your romantic past. You want to keep her focused on the present moment, on you and her.

Another baiting question we've heard involves the ménage à trois. Every guy has fantasized or at least wondered about getting it on with two women. There is a small percentage of women who are open to this idea, but most are *not* down with it. In fact, they may think you're a dog for even admitting that it turns you on.

If a girl asks you what you think about two-on-ones, no

matter how sexually liberated she may seem, don't take the bait. You run the risk of planting a poisonous seed in her mind, that you're a typical horny guy who's more interested in easy sex than committed relationships. Simply tell her, "I guess everyone fantasizes about it at some point, but I'd much rather be in a one-on-one relationship with someone that I can trust."

Another one they might ask is the cheating question: "Have you ever cheated on one of your girlfriends?" A lot of guys have fooled around during a relationship at least once in their life, and some are under the impression that it's okay to admit this. They may think they score points by being honest, or that it establishes that they're a stud.

Don't even think about it. It's never a good idea to talk about your past sexual conquests, whether it involved cheating or not. Shut this baiting question down by talking about the future instead: "I value loyalty a lot and I don't like disloyal people. But I don't worry about what you or I did in the past. Let's stay focused on the present and future."

Christopher once deflected the cheating question with a clever little story. He told the girl: "In the Mafia, it's traditional for guys to have their wives, and their 'goomahs'—y'know, their mistresses. But I heard a story once about a Mafia boss who looked down on the guys in his family who had goomahs. In fact, he had a hard time trusting them. His attitude was, 'How can you be loyal to this family if you can't be true to the one person in the world you vowed to be faithful to?'"

Instead of taking the girl's bait, he flipped it around and established that he valued loyalty. If the girl was suspicious before about his being a "player," she wasn't anymore.

Twenty-Minute Convo Rule

Not every conversation is going to lead to romance. Play it cool and see how things develop. Just follow this rule of thumb: if a girl talks to you for more than twenty minutes, it's officially more than just a casual encounter. No girl spends this much time talking to a guy if she thinks there is no romantic potential.

Once you've passed the twenty-minute mark, you should offer to buy her a drink if she is in need of one. At this point it's time to start working toward closing the deal, which we will discuss later.

Mack Fact: Seventy-three percent of men are still potent at age 70.

More Convo Basics

As a Mack, the game is not won or lost by how often you work out, or how good you look. Ultimately, it comes down to the words that come out of your mouth.

Believe us, there's a reason why Mack Commandment 8 is "Three-quarters of macking is listening." The more time you spend listening, the less chance you will say the wrong thing. As we're fond of saying, give a guy enough rope and he'll usually hang himself.

We can guarantee that you've done it at least once and not realized it—ruined a "sure thing" by saying something that suddenly cooled off a woman's attraction to you. We've heard a lot of women describe this scenario: a guy introduces himself, and based on his looks and the way he carries himself, she's interested.

At this point, he doesn't need to be brilliantly funny, or mention his high-powered job, or charm her pants off. She's hoping he can simply carry on a decent conversation, because that's all it will take for her to hook up with him. This guy is like a football team that's ahead by two touchdowns with five minutes left in the game. He doesn't need to make any spectacular plays; if he can just protect his lead and avoid making mistakes, victory is assured.

But more often than not, this guy will fumble the proverbial football and blow his lead. Most times he won't even realize where he went wrong. He might have thought he was being witty, while to the woman he came off as self-centered, chauvinistic, or even perverted. There is sometimes a great divide between what men and women think is "clever conversation."

Whenever you approach a woman and she is interested enough to begin conversing with you, you are a football team that is ahead in the fourth quarter. As you guide the conversation, you must protect your lead and avoid making boneheaded plays.

The following are some basic conversational "dos" and "don'ts":

Do humor her. If she's talking about subjects that interest her, let her talk and act genuinely interested. Give her a chance to shine.

Don't wait for your chance to jump in and talk about yourself.

Do ask her where she's originally from. It's an important piece of intel: is she from a big city, or is she a small-town girl with small-town values?

Don't try to guess what country a foreign woman is from. The chances of you guessing correctly on your first try are slim at best; the chances of you screwing it up are huge. In some cases, saying the wrong country might even insult her. If you're curious, your best bet is to say "You have a really striking look, where are your parents from?" Or, "Your accent is so cute. Where were you born?" (Asking this question also provides a gateway for you to segue into a conversation about travel.)

Do point out her positive qualities: "You know, Jennifer, I appreciate someone who's as ambitious as you are."

Don't use generalities when you're discussing men and women, i.e., "Women always get so jealous." Establish yourself as a person who judges others on their individual qualities. This way, you can call her on it if she makes unfair generalizations about men.

Women have a tendency to bunch us all together, saying things like, "All men are dogs," or, "Men are only interested in one thing." This is when you separate yourself from the Wack Pack and establish your respect for individuality: "I can understand why you would say that, but I try to judge people on their own merits."

This has a direct parallel to hostage negotiations. Hostage takers will frequently complain to the negotiator how "cops" always give them a hard time, or how "cops" accuse them of things because they've got a criminal record. In response to this, the negotiator separates himself from the "cop pack" in order to build one-on-one trust: "I can understand why you feel that way. If I were in your position, I'd feel the same. But this is your first time talking to me. I'm not judging you."

Do pay her original compliments, on an article of clothing or a piece of jewelry she is wearing.

Don't compliment her on her body, not even in a general sense (i.e., "I can tell you must work out.") Drawing attention to her body is either going to sound overtly sexual, or it's going to make her feel self-conscious. Wait until you've been intimate with her to comment on her more intimate aspects.

Finally, a few major "don'ts":

Don't brag about your sexual prowess, not even in jest. Don't mention how great you are in bed, your incredible stamina, how well endowed you are, or your tongue skills. Flirtatious sexual talk can be fun once you've gotten to know her. Coming from a stranger, the only future she's going to imagine with a guy like this involves a restraining order.

Don't make jokes about how you're *not* a psycho; they're not funny and they only turn her thoughts toward negative possibilities. While offering to give her a ride home, don't say anything like, "Don't worry, I'm not an axe murderer." We actually heard one guy say, while asking a girl out on a date, "I promise I won't kill you and dump your body in the woods." Needless to say, she wasn't available that weekend—or any weekend for the rest of her life.

Don't tell her she looks like a celebrity. You may think comparing her to Britney Spears or some TV actress is a compliment. But women are very particular about how they want men to perceive them. There is a chance she won't be flattered by the comparison and will get the wrong idea.

By telling her she reminds you of Jessica Simpson, you're trying to compliment her as a beautiful blonde—but she might infer that you think she's a ditz. By comparing her to J Lo, you're trying to compliment her sexy Latin looks—but she might think you've been ogling her sizeable booty. This is a game you will rarely win. Avoid celebrity comparisons.

A final note on this: if she really does bear a striking resemblance to a celebrity, you can bet this is something she hears on a regular basis and she's sick of it. Women want to be appreciated as individuals, not because they remind you of someone else.

Don't mention your ex, not even in the context of an innocent comment (i.e., "You were in Vegas recently? My ex and I went there once on vacation.") It makes you sound like you haven't been able to let go of her. More importantly, you want this girl to focus on what a future with you would be like. Your romantic past has no place in this conversation.

Don't complain. Even if you're doing it in a humorous context, don't complain about your boss, the jackass you had to deal with at work, how boring this party is, etc. Stay positive. If you've got a sarcastic sense of humor, dial it down. This might not be your favorite spot, but don't try to act "above" it. Remember, wherever *you're* at is the place to be.

Comfort Zones

When you approach a woman, she's in her own comfort zone. One of your primary goals as a Mack is to gently remove her from that comfort zone—without ever making her feel uncomfortable—and bring her into yours.

If you're in a crowded environment (such as a nightclub), bring her to an area where you can focus on conversation and on each other, rather than trying to talk over the music. If you can maneuver her to a bar or seating area near the exit, that is ideal. The subliminal implication is that you're already halfway there; the exit, which you plan to escort her through eventually, is just steps away.

Important Intel

In most cases, the goal of this first conversation is to lay the groundwork for a first date. This means that by the end of the conversation you need to have gathered certain pieces of key intel. They include:

- **What kind of food does she like?**
- **What is her work schedule?**
- **What are her days off?**
- **What does she like to do on her days off?**
- **Does she live alone, or with family or roommates?**
- **What part of town does she live in?**

By knowing this information, you will be properly equipped to ask her out on a date when the time comes. The chances of her saying no will be greatly reduced if you are aware of her schedule and what her interests are. But don't telegraph

your intentions; you don't want her to know that you're lead-
ing up to asking her out. If you want to find out her work
schedule, mention yours and then ask what hers is like. Work
it into the conversation.

Some guys will get a phone number, call the girl to try to
make plans with her for next Saturday night, and when she
says she'll be "busy" they take it as a rejection and never call
her again. If they'd bothered to find out that she *works* on
Saturday nights, they would have set things up for a different
evening and probably gotten a yes instead of a no.

Advanced Mack Maneuver: The 70/30 Rule

*The following is an entry from Christopher's Mack
Journal, found on www.macktactics.com.*

*Last night I hit one of the hottest clubs in Vegas
with my partner Rob. It was Thursday night, when
the place is always filled with hammers. (A "target-
rich environment," as we like to say.)*

*I noticed an exotic, dark-skinned hammer stand-
ing across the room by the dance floor. She was with
a friend who was far less attractive. I could tell they'd
come to the club together. (Have you ever noticed
how beautiful girls tend to travel with less-than-
beautiful friends? Must be an ego thing.) Normally
Rob would act as my wingman and distract the
wack friend, but he was already making his move
on some other fly girl. I'd have to do this one alone.*

I decided to use a M.A.C.K. Tactic designed for this exact situation. I'd make the wack friend my wingman without her even knowing it. (I call this technique "flipping," the same way the cops flip a bad guy, make him their informant, and use him to catch the big fish.)

So I walked over and introduced myself. It turned out the hammer was named Ashley: tall, beautiful smile, banging body. She introduced me to her friend, and I made sure I introduced myself to her in the same charming manner. I told her my name and gave her a nice smile and a warm handshake.

I knew what I had to do next. As we began chatting, I positioned my body toward the wack friend and pretended to be into her—more so than Ashley. I could tell by the way she was smiling, she wasn't used to getting this kind of attention. Especially not when she was out with Ashley.

I chatted with them both, getting some background details. They were college students visiting from California. They were staying at a nearby hotel, sharing a room, and had taken a cab over here because they heard it was a cool club.

I dropped a line: "I can't believe your boyfriends let you come to Vegas by yourselves." They giggled and assured me that they didn't have boyfriends.

They probably wouldn't admit it if they did, but I could tell by Ashley's body language that she was indeed single and available.

During this phase of the encounter, I maintained a 30/70 attention ratio. I paid attention to Ashley only 30 percent of the time, while giving the wack friend the rest of my attention. I was flirting with her, and she was loving it. She probably couldn't believe her luck—when was the last time a guy showed interest in her instead of gorgeous Ashley?

So now the friend is laughing at my jokes, flirting back. She's building me up in front of Ashley— acting as my wingman without knowing it. I could tell that this was putting Ashley on uncomfortable ground. This type of situation was foreign to her. She was trying to smile and be a part of the conversation, but I knew she was feeling jealous and ignored. All part of my strategy.

Now it was time for the first break point of the encounter. I asked them what kinds of drinks they wanted, then I went to the bar to get them. Obviously, the second I walked away they started talking about me behind my back.

Under normal circumstances, the guy (me) would have been hitting on Ashley, and the wack friend would start trying to discourage her: "He thinks he's all that, let's go to another club," etc.

But instead, because I flipped the friend, she's singing my praises while I'm at the bar. She's blowing me up, telling Ashley how great I am. Now Ashley's starting to feel competitive. She's also feeling self-conscious, wondering why I'm macking her friend instead of her!

Okay, now it's time to take care of business. When I return with the drinks, I shift to a 70/30 attention ratio. Now I'm giving Ashley the majority of my attention and starting to ignore her friend.

After I hand Ashley her drink, I do the "taste test." I ask her how it tastes, implying that I want to taste it myself. She hands me her drink. I go to put my lips on the straw, then smile and ask her if I'm going to get "cooties" from her. She laughs and says no. I take a sip from the straw and hand it back to her. Then she goes ahead and uses the straw.

The straw move is a very subtle technique that works with girls on a subliminal level. Now that we've swapped spit, a kiss won't be much of a leap.

At this point, I'm totally in control of the conversation. I'm breaking Ashley down and applying heavy Tactics. I'm locked in with eye contact and I'm guiding the conversation, talking about music, fashion, and travel . . . all stimulating subjects that we share common interests in. During this,

I'm still being polite to the wack friend and keeping her marginally involved. But it's obvious who I'm focusing on. My eye contact is locked in with Ashley.

It's too late for the friend to get between us. I've successfully removed her from the equation. At this stage, if the friend tries to pull Ashley away from me, or tries to bad-mouth me in any way, Ashley will think she's just being jealous.

Eventually, the friend takes the hint and tells us that she's going to go dance. Fine by us. She wanders off and leaves Ashley and me to get to know each other better. Now that I've reduced the situation to a one-on-one, it's time to apply more conversation control and move toward closing the deal.

Mack Fact: According to surveys by the condom company Durex, the worldwide average for sex is 106 times per year. Here's how some places stacked up between the sheets:

France:	141	Mexico:	102
U.S.A.:	138	Italy:	92
Russia:	131	Thailand:	80
Australia:	112	Hong Kong:	57
Canada:	105		

6

Hypotheticals

One of the most effective conversational tools in the M.A.C.K. Tactics arsenal is hypotheticals. These are hypothetical questions that you pose in the course of a conversation. A good one accomplishes a number of things. First, they're a great way to spark an interesting discussion. Second, they are an excellent means of gathering intel about her. Third, they allow you to highlight your own best qualities and tell her the qualities you value in a woman. Instead of stating these things outright, hypotheticals allow you to plant seeds in her brain that once again work in your favor.

Let's say you've been talking about music. She told you which bands she's into, and now you're telling her which ones you like. You know that in a matter of moments you're going to have to guide the conversation to the next topic, since it's important to keep things flowing. A hypothetical will catch her slightly off guard, make her smile and think, and open a whole new conversational gateway.

Hypothetical A: The Dinner Date

Here's a smooth one you can spring on her: "Okay, so let me ask you this. If you could have dinner with anyone, dead or alive, who would it be?"

The point here is to learn more about this girl and what makes her tick. If she answers with someone like Colin Farrell or Johnny Depp, you know she has a weak spot for bad boys who have an edgy style. If she says a politician's name, you know you're dealing with a girl who keeps up with current events and has strong opinions about world affairs. Whether this type of girl appeals to you or not, you've just gathered some important intel on her.

Regardless of who she says, be enthusiastic. If she gives a standard "chick" answer like Brad Pitt, laugh and say, "How did I know you were going to say that?" But don't let her off the hook that easy. Keep her mind working. Ask her "So what is it about him, besides the obvious physical things, that make him so intriguing to you?" The more detail she goes into, the more you learn. Maybe it's a particular movie he made. Find out.

She might pick someone unexpected and demonstrate that she is an independent thinker. If she has a clever answer, say, "That's interesting. So what is it about (insert name) that makes him so appealing to you?"

After she finishes explaining her choice, she'll probably turn the tables and ask you who your dinner date would be. Make sure you've done your homework before you use this hypothetical. You should already have several answers prepared, with reasons to back them up. Base your reply on the type of girl you're dealing with. If she picked a bad boy or anyone who leads an adventurous, free-spirited life, you could name a person who reflects those same qualities. If she would prefer to dine with someone who has a tremendous intellect, you could respond with a famous person who is known to be brilliant—whether it's in business, music, film, etc.—and has made a positive impact on the world.

You shouldn't have to be disingenuous and name someone you aren't actually interested in. Come up with several
people who have accomplished great things in different
fields, who you genuinely find fascinating. Then, when it's
your turn to answer the hypothetical, you can use the person that shares some of the same qualities as her choice.

When doing your homework and figuring out your
choices, think about two categories. Be ready with at least
one famous person who is in a strong, committed relationship; this shows the value you place on loyalty and commitment. Also, have someone who demonstrated tremendous
perseverance—someone who overcame great odds and became a success. Don't make obvious choices, but don't pick
people that most women won't be familiar with.

In the first category, an example would be David Bowie.
He's an amazing artist who has evolved and stayed on the
cutting edge through the decades. He's also married to the
supermodel Iman, who happens to be outside his race. Together, they make one of the world's most stylish couples.

In the second category, consider Tina Turner—a woman
who overcame a terribly abusive marriage, was relegated to
playing lounges and cheap gigs for years, but persevered
and fought her way to the top. Now in her sixties, she still has
huge sex appeal.

If you do give a famous woman as your answer, add some
icing to the cake by prefacing your choice: "I probably
wouldn't admit this in front of my guy friends, but there's
this woman I really admire . . ." This is just an additional
touch that shows you feel comfortable opening up to her.

Whatever your choice may be, have intelligent reasons
to support it. Explain why this person sparks your imagi-

nation and how you'd love the opportunity to ask certain questions.

A word of warning: you'll probably want to stay away from politics. Unless you're macking women at a political rally, this isn't the time to debate abortion laws or any other hot-button issues. Maintain the comfort zone. Keep things light, fun, and stimulating.

Hypothetical B: Cops at the Door

Loyalty is a quality that women, and Macks, take seriously. Here is an example of a hypothetical that allows you to (A) gauge how important loyalty is to her and (B) establish that you are loyal person.

This hypothetical should be used once you've established a connection. This could mean a second or third date. "Let me run this by you," you say with a sly smile. "It's a hypothetical situation."

"You've been dating a guy for a few weeks, and you really like him. One night you're at his house having dinner with him, and a police car pulls up outside. The guy suddenly jumps up and says to you, 'Tell them I'm not home.' Then he runs into the bedroom and hides in the closet.

"So the cops come knocking on the door. You answer. The cops ask you if he's home. What do you do? Do you lie and say he's not home? Or do you point them toward the bedroom?"

Girls will reveal a lot about themselves by the way they answer this question. If she says, "I'd cover for him," you know that she holds loyalty in high regard. When she cares about someone she has their back, and she's passionate with the men she loves. Therefore you need to play up how important these qualities are to you. Give a reply along these lines: "That's interesting that you would say that. Because honestly, if you flipped the situation, and I was dating you and I was the one answering the door . . . I would have to cover for you. Loyalty is at the top of my list."

If you want to rack up extra points, throw in a reference to the classic movie *Bonnie and Clyde* (1967). As a Mack, it's important that you watch this film and be able to tell girls about it. It's about a guy and a girl, played by Warren Beatty and Faye Dunaway, who fall madly in love and embark on a bank-robbing spree. They're fiercely loyal to each other; nothing can break them apart. It's them against the world, a notion that women find incredibly romantic.

A more modern reference is the movie *True Romance*, which was inspired by *Bonnie and Clyde*. This time it's Christian Slater and Patricia Arquette on the run, road-tripping from Detroit to Hollywood. Girls love this movie for the same reasons: two star-crossed lovers on the run, against all odds. *Bonnie and Clyde* ended on the more powerful note, with the two doomed lovers dying together in a hail of bullets—bloody, tragic, but still a very romantic notion.

Then again, she might give the opposite response to your hypothetical: "I'd tell the cops where he is. I haven't known the guy that long. What if he's a murderer or something, and didn't tell me?"

In this situation, you give an equally smooth reply: "I respect what you're saying. You believe in honesty, and if this guy wasn't being straight with you about himself, and what he's involved in, then there's no reason for you to cover for him. I also believe in honesty, I think it's very important."

For obvious reasons, you don't want to drop this hypothetical on a woman five minutes after you meet her. She might wonder whether you're trying to find a girl who really *will* cover for you when the cops come serving an arrest warrant. But once she knows you and you're enjoying some fun conversation, this one's a gem.

Hypothetical C: The Million-Dollar House

Another provocative question you can pose: "Okay, check this out. If I were to give you a million dollars to build your dream house, but you had to build it out of either wood, glass, or concrete, which material would you choose?"

The purpose here is to learn more about her personality. It also allows you to tell her how much you value certain qualities in women.

Once she gives her answer, compliment her on her answer. Whether she chose wood, glass, or concrete, say, "That's exactly what I thought you would say." Now you've got her intrigued. When she asks why, explain to her what her answer means about her. She'll be hanging on every word.

If she says "glass," tell her she's an open book. She's not afraid to reveal herself and what she's about. She has a wide circle of friends. People like to be around her.

If she answers "wood," tell her she's creative. She has artistic inclinations and likes to work with her hands.

If she answers "concrete," this is a person who needs to feel secure and puts a big value on stability. "It means you're very concerned about security," you tell her. "Not just your security, but that of the people close to you. And you want stability in your life. I can definitely appreciate that."

Most women who pick "concrete" have security issues because of a difficult relationship they've had in the past with a man. It could be her father; it could be an ex-boyfriend. Another piece of intel to file away.

All of these interpretations are broad enough that they apply to most women. But you should always be ready with a further explanation in the event that she disagrees with your interpretation. If she chooses glass, and you tell her she's an open person, she might say she's not: "Actually, I'm on the shy side. It takes me a while to open up to people." To this, you would say, "But I can tell that you want to be more open. You want to let people into your life, but something is holding you back." Now let her respond. A gateway has just opened to a personal, intimate discussion.

Likewise, if she chooses wood but tells you she's not creative, you can say, "But I can tell you've got a creative side you haven't really explored." Chances are she will be flattered by this statement and see truth in it. She'll probably find a reason to agree; maybe she has an interest in art, or would love to learn how to play a musical instrument, but hasn't explored these areas. As she shares these personal details about herself, the bond between you and her is strengthened.

Hypothetical D: Age Is Just a Number

"My friends and I were talking about this the other day, and I'm curious what you think. Which do you think is more appropriate: an older guy with a much younger girlfriend, or a young guy dating a much older woman?"

Notice that you phrased this politely by using the word "appropriate." You didn't pass judgment on either option.

This hypothetical opens a gateway for you to discuss life, vitality, fun, and enjoying love at any age. No matter how she answers, you can establish that you believe in the concept of true love and living life to the fullest.

She might say, "I think it's gross when I see an old man with a twenty-year-old."

To this, you say something along the lines of: "I'll admit, it does look a little strange. But look at the deeper part of it: if they're in love with each other, and they make each other's lives better, does age really matter?"

On the other hand, if she says, "Age shouldn't matter, as long as they're in love," then you should wholeheartedly agree. If your parents or grandparents have been married for many years, or you can relate a sweet story about a couple that you know that has been together forever, tell her about it. Women find this notion very romantic. You can't go wrong with this hypothetical; every woman has an opinion on it, and it opens excellent conversational gateways.

Hypothetical E: The Five Senses

Women tend to be more sensual than men. They have a deeper appreciation for breathtaking scenery, soothing sounds, and gentle caresses. Since romance is about stimulating a woman's senses, here is a hypothetical that opens gateways to romantic and sensual subjects:

"If you had to lose one of your senses—sight, sound, smell, taste, or touch—which is the one you would never want to give up?"

It's a tricky question that will make her think for a moment. Her answer isn't the point. It's all about you asking her *why* that sense is so important to her, and taking it from there.

She might say, "I would never want to lose my hearing. I love music, I couldn't live without it."

So now you know she's a big music fan. This is valuable intel; you can discuss music with her, a topic she obviously enjoys talking about, and a great first date with her could involve going to hear some live music.

The same principle applies to whichever sense she says. Maybe she values her sight above all others, because she couldn't imagine never seeing another sunset. Perhaps she would choose to keep her sense of touch. What are the things she would miss touching? Here's a perfect opportunity for you to stress how you're an affectionate person, and you could never live without touch, either. You can say, "Touch has to be the most powerful of all the senses. It's amazing what it can do. I could be having a terrible day, feeling really down, and a simple touch from someone I love can heal everything." Give her forearm a gentle touch while you say this.

Whatever her answer is, say, "I can understand why you feel that way." Have your own answer prepared: which sense is most important to you? It should tell her something about you and the things you value most.

By playing upon her senses, you develop a romantic bubble around the two of you. You are communicating and connecting on a level that goes way beyond normal conversation.

Hypothetical 7: The Voyeur

This one is flirtatious and a lot of fun. Don't use it until the two of you have established a good connection. You need to be enjoying each other's company, and she needs to be relaxed. If she has a strong sexual energy—i.e., she's dressed provocatively and is partying it up—this one can open a lot of doors.

Say, "Let me ask you a hypothetical question." Or, if you've already asked her one of the above questions, say, "Okay, how 'bout one more hypothetical." (It is hard to get tired of these; it feels like the two of you are playing your own private game.)

"Let's say you've just moved into a new place, and you realize that you can see into the house across the street from you. A guy and a girl live there, both very attractive people. One night you look through your blinds and you see them making mad, passionate love. (Don't call it 'sex.') They're so into each other, there's no way they're going to notice you. So the question is this: do you close your blinds, or do you watch?"

With this one, you're steering the conversation into sexual territory. As long as the chemistry between you is good, she will find this question sexy, intriguing, and a bit naughty—in a good way.

There is no wrong answer. Again, the key is to ask her why she answers the way she does. If she says, "I wouldn't look. I think sex is something that two people should share privately," you might say, "What is it that would stop you from looking? I'm not saying that I would look, but what would hold you back?" Allow her to explain her view of sex. Now *there* is some highly valuable Mack intel.

If she gave a prudish answer, say, "I'm not going to lie to you; curiosity would probably get the better of me. But I would think 'how would I feel if someone was watching me?' I do think it's a personal thing between two people." This way, you're establishing that you have a sexual side while still agreeing with her.

On the other hand, she might admit that she would watch. This means you're dealing with a sexual person and there are some nice possibilities. You can use the same statement as above; curiosity would get the better of you, but you're no Peeping Tom.

This is not about trying to get her to talk dirty; trying to blatantly steer the conversation into sexual territory is a Wack Tactic. You are gauging her level of sexuality, gathering intel, and continuing to be original with your conversation.

More Hypotheticals

Here are some quick hypothetical questions that can go a long way. Any time you ask a woman one of the following questions, she will reveal something about herself.

If could you teleport right now to any place in the world, where would you go?

Which would you rather have for one day: the power to fly or the power to be invisible?

If Hollywood makes a movie about your life one day, which actress would you want playing you?

If you could eat one food as much as you want and never gain a single ounce, what would it be?

If you could gaze into a crystal ball and see a single day in your future, which day would you want to see?

What's the best purchase you've ever made?

Mack Fact: In the Dominican Republic you can get a divorce in one day.

Negotiations

This is the core of M.A.C.K. Tactics, a set of principles that were literally gained through blood, sweat, and tears on the battlefield—the kind where bullets fly, instead of Cupid's arrows. Here we'll explain the powerful connection between hostage negotiation and the art of macking.

The Negotiator Mind-set

The negotiator is a calming, nonthreatening presence. He conveys the sense that he is the hostage taker's ally, the one person in the world who is willing to listen and make sure everything works out. But the negotiator is always the one in control. He's like an actor who has memorized the script; he already knows how it's going to end, it's simply a matter of steering it there.

Now, let's put this in Mack terms. If you're the negotiator, and the female you're scoping is the hostage taker, who's the hostage? The answer, for most men, is their confidence. The bottom line is that women have hijacked our cojones and they've already got their demands worked out. We, as men, are eager to recapture our confidence from them. So we acquiesce to their demands—in small ways when we first meet them, and in profound ways once we're committed to a relationship or marriage. Surrendering is always much easier than standing your ground.

As most men know, the demands of women never cease. Oftentimes, they don't even need to verbalize their demands; men rush to provide them with whatever they might need. We pay for the drinks. We take them out on dates, wining and dining them and trying to play the perfect gentleman. We listen to them talk about problems. And we do all this wearing a phony smile, figuring if we put in enough time and jump through enough hoops, maybe she'll reciprocate and satisfy our physical needs—allowing us to recapture some of the self-confidence we lost along the way.

The Mack doesn't play this game. He deals with women like a hostage negotiator deals with a hostage taker: operating from a playbook, using strategies to achieve his end goal no matter how long it takes. He'll do what it takes to win the encounter, and has the patience and self-discipline to see his plan through.

Imagine a scenario where a hostage taker says, "I need a plane, $50,000, and a passport so I can leave the country." If you were to watch this scenario unfold, and the negotiator acquiesced to every one of those demands, you would think he was a fool. Yet most men normally make constant concessions to women.

In a hostage situation, the hostage taker may think he's the one calling the shots. But in the negotiator's mind, there are only two options: you're either going deal with me and work things out my way, or we "go tactical" and the SWAT team takes you down.

If you initiate an encounter with a woman but she's on guard, throwing up barriers and being standoffish, approach it the way a hostage negotiator would. While you're never going to go "tactical" on her, you are going to approach the encounter with two options firmly planted in your mind. As far as you're concerned, it's going to work out one of two ways:

Option #1: She may have issues going on in her life right now, but you're going to find ways to get past them. You're going to break down the barriers so the two of you can have a good time together.

Option #2: Even after making your best attempt, you are unable to reach a happy medium with her. For whatever reason, she just isn't interested in building a bridge with you. No hard feelings. The two of you will go your separate ways, and you'll work your magic on someone who is more responsive to your time and energy. You also know that even during that brief encounter, you were able to practice your tactics and note a detail or two that adds to your overall knowledge of women.

Empower yourself with these thoughts. Forget about rejection; there is no such thing. There are ideal outcomes, and then there are outcomes that free you up to mack other women—leaving you more knowledgeable than before. You will either work out a deal with her, or you will find someone who is willing to meet your terms.

IOUs

The book *Crisis Negotiations* by Michael McMains and Wayman Mullins, used by major police departments across the country, refers to the "rule of reciprocity." This rule means that if you do a favor for someone, they will feel obliged to repay the favor. It's basic human nature. When you do something nice for a woman, even if it's something simple that you would do for anyone, you want to reinforce in her mind that you've just done her a favor. Therefore, she will feel that she should reciprocate on some level. In *M.A.C.K. Tactics*, we refer to this technique as creating "IOUs."

Let's say the hostage taker, call him "Bob," is holed up in an apartment. It's the dead of winter, freezing temperatures. Early in the standoff, the negotiator tells him, "I just want you to know, Bob, I'm going to make sure right now that no one's going to mess with the electricity. I'm going to make sure your heat stays on so you're comfortable in there."

In reality, the cops had no intention of cutting off his heat. Maybe there are kids in the apartment with Bob; maybe the cops don't even have access to the electricity. Yet Bob thinks the negotiator has made an extra effort to look out for him. As the negotiator continues to do Bob "favors" (the next one being, "I'm going to make sure none of these officers out here hurt you"), Bob begins to trust and appreciate the negotiator. The negotiator has become his fellow traveler, his ally in a stressful situation.

When the negotiator then asks for reciprocity (i.e., "I've been helping you out, Bob, now I need you to free one of those hostages"), Bob is much more likely to listen and respond in a positive manner. He might not be ready to surrender yet, but he doesn't want to lose his only ally.

In *M.A.C.K. Tactics*, we use this same principle. When a man approaches a woman and tries to initiate a conversation, the woman's stress levels naturally rise. Thoughts and questions are running through her mind: Who is this guy? What does he want? Her brain is trying to interpret a hundred different signals he is sending her way, from his body language to his facial expression to the things he is saying and doing. The unskilled guy will say and do things that increase her stress levels and her doubts about him. The Mack puts her in a comfort zone and becomes her fellow traveler.

The minimal encouragers we outlined in chapter 5 will help in this regard. Keep the conversation flowing, listen attentively, and express interest in what she has to say. This keeps her stress levels at a minimum while gradually increasing her comfort level with you.

Special Efforts

The Mack is always in negotiator mode with regard to women, whether it's the initial conversation or a fourth date. Anything she asks for is technically a demand, and when the Mack chooses to meet one of those demands he does not allow it to be taken for granted—just as when a hostage taker requests a cigarette, the negotiator makes it clear that he is making a special effort by arranging for one.

As a Mack, you do this in a subtle way. This doesn't mean you lay guilt trips on her every time you do the slightest thing for her. You don't make a big deal out of the fact that you paid for her drink or her meal. But when you give her these things, you use creative phrasing to reinforce in her mind that (A) she has earned it, and (B) you are making an effort that you wouldn't make for any ordinary girl.

Wack Tactic: "Can I buy you a drink?"
Mack Tactic: "I'm really enjoying getting to know you. I'd like to go ahead and buy you a drink."

Most guys shell out for drinks because they feel they're supposed to. The Mack implies that she has *earned* the drink because he is enjoying her company.

Setting Precedents

The average guy downplays it when he does something nice for a woman. If he drives across town through a blinding rainstorm to give her a ride home, when she thanks him he'll say, "No problem. Anytime." If she asks him to help her move to a new apartment, which means lugging furniture all day in the sweltering heat, he'll say, "Sure, I'll be free this weekend." If he digs deep to pay for an expensive date that is beyond his budget, he'll say, "No big deal. It was my pleasure."

He *thinks* he's playing it cool by downplaying his efforts. But this is setting a bad precedent. The woman will come to expect this level of treatment and attention. The gestures she once appreciated, she comes to expect. Her demands will escalate over time, and as they rise his power will diminish.

The Mack knows the correct way to deal with a woman's demands. He is consistently generating IOUs, reinforcing in her mind that he is going above and beyond the call of duty. He's doing things for her that deserve reciprocation.

IOUs come in all shapes and sizes. Let's say you're sitting at home on a Friday night, watching TV. You don't have any particular plans. Then the phone rings: it's a hammer who you met the other night. You would love to see her again.

She asks what you're doing. To this, the average guy might respond, "Nothing, just watching TV. What are you up to?" He's hoping that she is free tonight and wants to make plans.

The Mack might be hoping the same thing, but he puts a spin on it and turns it into an IOU. "I had a long day at work," he says. "I rented some movies and I was just going to chill. Why, what are you doing?"

She says she's going to a bar with a couple of friends: does he want to join them? The Mack takes a moment, as if considering it. He replies, "You know what? I was going to take tonight off and relax, but it would be nice to see you. Maybe I could come meet you for an hour."

Note the difference. Instead of admitting that he's home alone in front of the boob tube, he just made plans with the girl *and* established in her mind that he's doing it because *she's worth making the special effort.* In her view, he's changing his plans to spend some time with her. When he shows up at the bar, she's appreciative—instead of feeling like she did him a favor, inviting him to come out when he had nothing better to do.

The Mack can create another IOU at the end of the night, when he's walking her to her door: "I was only planning on staying out for an hour, but I was having such a good time with you that I thought it was worth missing some sleep."

If she had a good time with him at the bar, there is now a much higher probability that she will invite him inside—and perhaps pay him back for his efforts.

The Mack never misses an opportunity to create an IOU. Consider this little one: when you walk into a restaurant with a girl and go to sit down at a table, ask her which side she would prefer to sit on. No matter which side she picks, you smile and say, "That's funny, that's the side I always sit on." She'll say, "Oh, that's okay, you take that side then," but you gently insist that she take it.

It makes no difference to you which side of the table you sit on. But on a subliminal level, you've "given" her something. While it is of no value to you, she feels that you've extended yourself.

IOUs add up. If she is made to feel that you are constantly doing little things for her, she is far more likely to reciprocate the way you want her to.

Another great thing about IOUs is that they create a

"safety net" when it's time for you to make your move. When the Mack goes for a good-night kiss, he knows that if she hesitates it's time to cash one in.

"Wow," he says jokingly. "I let you take my favorite seat at dinner, and I can't even get a kiss." She'll smile at this clever, unexpected comment, and might reconsider that kiss. The rule of reciprocity in action.

Life Applications

IOUs can translate into all areas of your life. We have opportunities to create them every day with our friends, bosses, even our parents—anyone who calls upon us to do things.

An example would be someone calling you to discuss some business. A standard question they might ask is, "Am I catching you at a bad time?" The typical response to that would be, "No, not at all," even if you're busy doing something else. It just seems like the proper thing to say.

Instead, create an IOU: "I've got a lot on my plate right now, but I'm going to put it aside for a few minutes. Let's talk." Now you're starting this business conversation from a position of power. Your time is valuable and scarce, but you're willing to give him some. He now feels a sense of pressure to make this phone conversation worthwhile for you.

If a girl says, "I'll call you later," instead of just saying okay, turn it into an IOU. Tell her, "I was planning on relaxing tonight and watching a movie, so I wasn't going to answer my phone. But I do want to speak with you, so I'll look out for your call."

Start creating them at your job as well. Let's say you're

about to go home for the day, but your boss suddenly drops an assignment on your desk. He asks if you can finish up this extra work before you leave—but you know, and he knows, that it isn't a request. It's a polite demand.

Instead of saying, "Sure, no problem," a well-spoken IOU creates a different impression in his mind: "I know that you need this taken care of, so I'm going to stay until it gets done." With that simple sentence, you're sending the message that you're a team player who recognizes the importance of the assignment. Earn the bonus points you deserve, rather than acting like a drone who simply does whatever task is handed to you.

Adopt this mind-set. It can be applied in endless ways. People will begin to view you as someone whose time is precious, but you are generous enough to make time for them.

Gifts

Ever since Eve gave Adam the apple, there has been a misunderstanding between the sexes about gifts.
—Nan Robertson

*Men who have pierced ears
are better prepared for marriage.
They've experienced pain and bought jewelry.*
—Rita Rudner

Gifts are another form of IOUs. Most men take a backward approach to the idea of gift-giving. They give women things in the hopes of getting something in the future, when the gift *should* be a "thank-you" for something she has already done.

Wack Tactic: giving her flowers before your first date, in the hopes of getting some action at the end of the night.
Mack Tactic: the first time you met her, you found out who her favorite author is. You wind up going on a date, and it goes well. Before your second date, you buy one of that author's books and give it to her. This gesture shows that you were attentive, and it's much more original than flowers. When she thanks you, you imply that the book is a *reward*: "I had a great time with you the other night, so I just wanted to get you a little something."

As a Mack, you will no longer give gifts in an attempt to score points with women. You give them because she earned them: she was on time for your date the other night, she looked great, and she was enjoyable to spend time with. This is a far more empowering mind-set. You are the one meting out the rewards, not the other way around.

Demands

The negotiating process always involves demands. In every situation, the negotiator knows going in that there will be negotiable demands and non-negotiable demands. The hostage taker can rant all he wants about getting a 747 to Cuba, but the negotiator knows that it is not an option. Other non-negotiable demands would include weapons or drugs. When the hostage taker demands these things, the negotiator won't flat-out say no; this will only aggravate the situation. Instead, the negotiator steers the conversation in another direction. "Why do you want that plane?" he might ask. This will prompt the hostage taker to start explaining the reasons behind his request: he's afraid of being killed by the cops, his wife has abandoned him, he lost his job, etc. When he opens up about his problems, the negotiator can lend a sympathetic ear, assure him that those problems are going to be worked out, and build a bridge of trust.

Conversely, the negotiator knows there are certain demands that he will agree to—*if* the hostage taker earns them. Negotiable demands may include food, cigarettes, and water. Though they are simple requests, the negotiator always makes the hostage taker feel that a special effort is being made to grant these demands. Quid pro quo: I've just done something for you, now I expect you to do something for me. I made sure you got something to drink; now I need you to let one of those hostages come outside.

As it becomes clear to the hostage taker that no 747 is forthcoming, he will scale down his demands to more manageable ones. But the negotiator does not grant any demand right away, because by doing so he relinquishes power. Instead, he stalls by asking more questions and keeping him talking. This way, if and when he grants a demand, it takes on greater significance: "You know what, John? You've been talking to me, telling me what you're going through, and I appreciate that. So I'm going to make sure you get some food now."

As a Mack, you must always know up front which demands you are willing to meet—how much you are willing to give in order to accomplish your end goal. Any request from a woman that involves an expenditure of your time and/or money should be viewed as a demand. Be wary of granting any demand from a woman too quickly. Even if you intend to give it to her, you'll make the gesture more significant by holding it back for a while.

For instance, a girl you've been seeing mentions that she's heard about a great new seafood restaurant. She's not telling you outright, "Take me to dinner there," but she's implying that she wants it. The average guy, eager to score points, will immediately offer to do so.

The Mack is more calculating. He makes a Mack Mental Note (MMN) of this, and sometime in the future he surprises her by taking her to that seafood restaurant. Now she feels that she is being rewarded. It's not a particularly expensive place; he could have taken her there for dinner at any point. But by holding back, then granting the demand when he feels it is appropriate to do so, he is asserting control and "rewarding" her instead of simply doing the expected. Ordinary men do what is expected. Macks do things on their own terms.

Sometimes these demands are on your time. If you begin dating a woman but have a busy schedule, set parameters in your mind about how much time you are willing to devote to her. Then, stick to them. She may complain about wanting to spend more time with you, but you have established a non-negotiable demand and she has no choice but to respect it. The nights that you do spend with her will feel more like special occasions. She knows that your time is in short supply, and she will appreciate your company rather than expect it.

If she wants you to spend every Saturday night with her, but you want the option to hang out with your buddies, establish that you won't always be available on that night of the week. Be nice about it, but let her know that your friends are important to you and you don't get much time to spend with them. This puts you in a position of control. From this point forward, every Saturday night that you *do* spend with her is a bonus. Instead of relinquishing control and apologizing for not being able to see her, you are increasing your power.

Other times, the demands are on your wallet. Before you go on a date, set a limit on what you are comfortable spending. If she asks you to take her to a fancy restaurant, only do so if you've decided beforehand that it is within your parameters. If you're not comfortable with the idea of spending a lot money on dinner, suggest a more casual, less expensive place instead. If things go well, you may decide to take her to the fancy place on a future date. If and when that happens, she will feel that you are doing something special for her, and be more appreciative. She will feel that she earned that dinner. Never allow her to take you, or your wallet, for granted.

This isn't about saving a few bucks. This is about respecting yourself. When you set these parameters in your mind, you are telling yourself that you are in charge of the situation and the outcome. Otherwise, you won't earn respect from her and will lose respect for yourself.

Christopher recalls a story about a negotiation that had been dragging on for hours. The hostage taker, speaking to the negotiator over a phone line, kept asking for a cigarette. The negotiator stalled until he felt it was time to accommodate the request. He then had a single cigarette delivered to the hostage taker.

Seconds later, the hostage taker called the negotiator back, freaking out, saying he needed a light. The negotiator calmly replied, "What you asked for was a cigarette. If you want a match, we'll deal with that next."

Approach Parameters

Parameters should also be used when making an approach. Let's say you spot a pretty girl sitting alone in a coffee shop. You want to join her at her table and start a conversation.

> **Wack Tactic:** "Is anyone sitting here? Do you mind if I join you?"
>
> **Mack Tactic:** "Hi, my name is Christopher. I have a few minutes and I'd like to meet you."

The first option may sound like the normal way of going about it, but the second is far more effective. Why? Because you have established a set of parameters for the encounter that is about to follow.

With the Mack Tactic, you are sending a series of messages to her. First, you are introducing yourself by name. This establishes that you are a confident person and feel comfortable with the package you are presenting to her. Second, the phrase "I have a few minutes" implies that you are a busy person, but would like to spend a few minutes of your time getting to know her. (If she's busy or uninterested, this also makes your exit much more graceful; you were only planning on giving her "a few minutes.")

Looking ahead, if you do join her and things go well, you

can remind her at some point that you were only planning to chat for a few minutes (a fact you established up front), but the conversation is so interesting that you decided to stay. She'll appreciate this bit of flattery, and you've just racked up an IOU. The message you're sending is that she's not giving you her time. You're giving her yours.

See how much information and strategy you can pack into one simple sentence? Now let's look at why the wack approach is filled with negative connotations:

Him: "Is anyone sitting in that chair?"
Her: "Uh . . . no, no one's sitting there."
Him: "Do you mind if I join you?"

By failing to introduce himself by name, the wack guy immediately generates negative suspicions in her mind. She's not thinking a guy named Christopher would like to spend a few minutes meeting her (a harmless-sounding proposition); she's wondering who this stranger is and what his deal is. His intentions are unknown. If she lets him sit down, is he going to try to talk her ear off for the next hour? Is he going to try to sell her something? By using an ambiguous approach, he has placed multiple obstacles in his own path.

Christopher, on the other hand, clearly stated his intentions: he has a few spare minutes and he would like to meet her. Though the two approaches may sound similar, there is a world of difference.

Additionally, Christopher gathered some quick intel before he made the approach. He took note of the way she's dressed and the book that she is reading. These are all launching pads for conversation. As soon as he sits down, he can go to work with an effective game plan.

Getting Past No

As you learned in the "Conversation Control" chapter, phrasing is everything. Good negotiators are masters of phrasing. There are so many times in life when we could get a yes, but get a no instead because we phrased the request the wrong way.

When you approach a girl, she has a million reasons to say no. In fact, she's probably looking for reasons to say it. These reasons could be beyond your control. You might look sort of like her ex, or remind her of her boss, or even her absentee father. She might be coming off a bad relationship. If you're at a nightclub, perhaps she has convinced herself that it's impossible to meet a decent guy in that environment, that they're all creeps and pickup artists.

Most women have programmed themselves to say no, and if you give them the opening they often will. Creative phrasing is how you overcome this. One example is the Mack method we've given for getting her phone number. When you simply ask, "Can I call you sometime?" her mind considers the negative possibilities (you might start calling her constantly) before considering the positive ones (you might be a great guy).

This is why the correct phrase would be, "I remember you told me you're off on Saturdays. When would be the best time for me to call you?"

This request (A) utilizes your intel, (B) shows that you

were attentive during the conversation, and (C) requires more than a yes or no answer, making it more difficult for her to turn you down. It also incorporates all four pillars of M.A.C.K. Tactics. You have applied method, taken action, shown confidence, and used knowledge.

As the Mack says this phrase he takes out his cell phone, like he's ready to program in her number. He has stated his intention: that he is going to call her when it's a good time for him to do so. If the last guy annoyed her by calling three times the next day, the Mack has eliminated that concern. He's laying out the terms of the deal: you tell me the time, and I'll call you then.

Also note that he didn't ask for permission. This phone call is *going to happen*. The actual act of her telling him her number is reduced to a minor detail, something they'll take care of in a moment.

To ensure a yes answer, the Mack has also laid the proper groundwork. By using effective conversation control up to this point, he has made her feel comfortable with him. The Mack has guided her down the "yes" path instead of creating opportunities for "no."

You will encounter scenarios where there are obstacles you aren't aware of. Let's say the girl recently went through a painful breakup and made a pledge to herself that she wouldn't get involved with anyone new for a while. She doesn't tell you any of this, but it's an invisible obstacle to your success.

By building a bridge of trust during the conversation, you eliminate barriers like these and crack open the door to romantic possibilities. Just don't get overconfident and deviate from your tactics. Stay on course. If you're not careful, the point where you attempt to get her phone number is when she might suddenly remember her "no new guys" pledge and turn you down. Never assume that you're "in" with her and will get her number no matter how you phrase the question. Follow Mack strategy from start to finish.

Preemptive Actions

There are all kinds of ways for women to say no and a million different reasons for them to say it, whether you're trying to get a phone number or inviting them back to your place. It's natural for them to have doubts and concerns about a guy they just met. During your conversation, you can lay groundwork that will negate some of the most common doubts and concerns. In *M.A.C.K. Tactics*, this is known as taking "preemptive actions."

For instance, some women will say, "I don't know, I just met you," if you invite them back to your place. This means they either have suspicions about you or might feel guilty about hooking up with a guy they barely know. You can plant seeds during the conversation to reduce these concerns. Once you start vibing and discover you have things in common, you can say, "It's funny, I feel like we've known each other a while, like we've met before. Do you feel the same way?" Even though you did just meet her, you're planting the seed that it doesn't *feel* that way.

She might wind up saying, "I just got out a relationship, I'm not ready." Eliminate this concern by planting seeds earlier on, with a general statement: "People should live in the moment, don't you think? Too many people dwell on what happened to them in the past."

If things get to the hot-and-heavy stage, she might shut you down with the statement, "Sex is special to me." Again, this form of "no" can be avoided by laying down groundwork earlier in the evening. Reinforce in her mind that she is special to *you*, and you are doings things for her that you don't normally do with women. When taking her to a restaurant, say, "This restaurant is one of my special places, I don't usually bring people here." Or mention, "My house is like my sanctuary, I almost never bring people there." This way, when she winds up back at your place she already feels like a special guest. Make her feel like a VIP in your world.

I Can't Go for That

It takes a woman twenty years
to make a man of her son,
and another woman
twenty minutes to make a fool of him.
—Helen Rowland

The average guy, while trying to score points with a girl, is willing to do things that he really doesn't want to do. He worries that saying no to one of her requests will cause her to think less of him. If he's in a long-term relationship with her, saying no could trigger an argument that he'd rather not deal with. Some guys figure it's easier to just bite their tongue and reach for their wallet.

There are situations where you *will* have to grin and bear

it. There has to be a degree of give-and-take for any relationship to work. You might prefer a baseball bat to the groin over shelling out for Justin Timberlake concert tickets, but you take her because she really wants to go. You might want to watch the NFL playoffs, but you accompany her to her sister's baby shower because it would mean a lot to her.

These are examples of things you would do for a woman once you are in a relationship. But in the early stages, as you are getting to know each other, it is imperative that you are willing to say no. It's a matter of establishing parameters. Furthermore, in these early stages you need to make the best possible impression every time you're with her. When you are uncomfortable and have no control over the environment, you're not at your best as a Mack. If she proposes an activity that puts you in this type of situation, you should politely decline.

Let's say you've got plans to take a girl out dancing. You're looking forward to a fun, one-on-one evening. This will be a second date, and you made these plans with her a week ago.

But when you call her to set a time for you to pick her up, she suddenly tries to switch the plans. She says that a bunch of her coworkers are going out to a karaoke bar and she wants to know if the two of you can go there instead.

You have zero interest in karaoke. You can't carry a tune to save your life, and her coworkers from the accounting firm are probably about as much fun as oral surgery. If you go, you know you're going to have a lousy time. Plus, tonight is your second date with her. This means that strategically, it's an important evening. You want it to take place in an environment where you can be at your best.

The average guy would reply to her request (which is really more like a demand) in one of two ways: either by bending ("Sure, we can go there instead") or by getting agitated ("I thought we were going out dancing. Why do you want to go to some stupid karaoke bar?").

Either way, his night is shot. He'll either go to the karaoke bar and feel like a third wheel, or she'll go out dancing with him as originally planned—but she'll be in a rotten mood because of the way he shot down her suggestion.

Instead, play it like a Mack and deny the demand with some positive spin: "That sounds like a good time, but I'd rather see you when I can have your undivided attention. You go out with your friends tonight and have a good time. Give me a call tomorrow and let me know how it turned out."

Here, not only are you saving yourself time, money, and aggravation—the karaoke bar would have cost you all three—you're also showing her that you're not a controlling person. You're comfortable letting her do her own thing.

Setting these parameters with a woman early in a relationship will pay off down the line. If she knows you simply *will not do* certain things, she'll know better than to nag you about them. And if you have no objections to her going out with friends—especially friends of the opposite sex—there shouldn't be a problem when you want to do the same.

Negotiation Principles

William Ury's book *Getting Past No* contains a five-step model for hostage negotiators to follow. It has direct applications to macking. (For simplicity's sake, we combined the fourth and fifth principles.)

1. Go to the balcony. The negotiator doesn't go anywhere in a literal sense. It means he "steps outside of himself" and imagines being up above, looking down on the scenario. This is a psychological technique that helps negotiators maintain their cool. They must remain calm and keep a level of emotional detachment. If the negotiator becomes angry or overly sympathetic, he might deviate from his game plan and act with his heart instead of his head.

Likewise, a woman might do or say things that get under your skin. Before you react, "go to the balcony" and imagine yourself watching your conversation from a third-party perspective. Think about why she's saying these things. Consider what you've done to trigger her behavior. Refocus your game plan.

Sometimes men fall into the opposite trap: they start thinking about how well they're doing and become overly confident. A guy might think, "This girl is *so* into me," and figure it's no longer necessary to stick with his tactics. He starts running his mouth when he should be listening, or allowing her to guide the conversation to places it shouldn't go (such as talking about his ex-girlfriends). He forgets that one false move can shatter the bridge that he has been building.

The next time you're macking a female, try taking the balcony view for a moment. Imagine that you're watching yourself talk to her. What is your body language saying? What is hers saying? What are the topics that make her smile and open up? Are there any subjects that it seems she'd rather not get into? Are you making progress, or are you treading water?

2. Step to her side. In most hostage situations, the hostage taker is severely pissed off at someone or something. The negotiator must make him feel as though they're traveling down the same road together. He understands what the guy is going through and would feel the same way if he was in his shoes.

This is the same approach the Mack takes when he is trying to get to know a woman, but she is irritated or upset about something. Her negative mood is a barrier he must remove. According to Ury's model, this is accomplished with a three-step approach: listen, identify with what the the hostage taker is feeling, and acknowledge it.

Let's say the hostage taker has been ranting about how his wife left him for the mailman. The negotiator says, "I know that must have hurt. But you know what? Since you've been willing to tell me some things about you that are very personal, I want to do something for you now. I'm going to talk to my guys out here, and make sure no one comes in there after you."

Putting this in Mack terms, let's say you're trying to build a bridge with a hammer, but she keeps complaining about her boss and his lewd sexual comments. Because of this, she has formed an opinion that "all men are dogs; they're only interested in sex." Obviously this is a barrier you need to remove in order to connect with her.

Don't point out that "you're not like most men." This is something you need to make her feel through your actions. Don't challenge what she is saying or try to stand up for your fellow man. And you certainly shouldn't interject with your own anecdote about someone you know who was sexually harassed. Just *listen* to what she is saying. Let her words and feelings flow.

Next, *identify* with her feelings and become her fellow traveler: "I can tell it really upsets you when someone treats you like that. If I was put in that situation, I'd feel the same way."

Finally, the Mack *acknowledges* that while he sympathizes with her situation, the present moment is what matters most: "I completely understand how you feel. But you know what? You're not at your office right now. You came out tonight to enjoy yourself, so let's do that."

3. Change the game. Next, move the discussion to another subject. You've allowed her to vent, you've empathized, but now it's time to move on—just as the negotiator doesn't want the hostage taker to dwell on his cheating wife, since it will only make him more upset.

Make this next topic something fun and

interesting. Now is a good time to discuss one of your favorites, or pose a hypothetical that takes her mind completely off her problem.

4./5. Build a golden bridge. / Make it hard to say no. Negotiators sometimes refer to this as "building a bridge of yesses." They never want to make it easy for the hostage taker to say the word "no," because that puts the hostage taker in a position of power.

If the negotiator asks, "Will you come outside now?" the hostage taker can easily refuse. He has a million reasons not to come outside. He's worried about being shot by the cops, getting shipped off to prison, etc. He can only imagine worst-case scenarios.

Instead, the negotiator will pose a question that addresses the hostage taker's concerns. He might ask, "What would happen if you came out right now?"

This question prompts the hostage taker to voice his specific concerns: "If I come out there, I'm going to get shot."

Now the negotiator has something he can work with. He can ease this concern by explaining exactly what *will* happen: "No one's going to rush you or hurt you. You and me are going to sit down in my car and talk about your problem." To the hostage taker, surrendering peacefully might now sound like an option.

Compare this to a macking situation, in which a

girl is reluctant to give you her phone number. "I'm not looking to date anyone right now," she says. Or "Sorry, I don't give out my phone number to people I don't know."

So you respond by posing this question: "What do you think would happen if I gave you my phone number?"

The question catches her off guard. She's not sure where you're going with this. "I don't know," she says.

Now you lay out a scenario that addresses and eliminates her concerns: "Here's what's going to happen. I'm going to call you tomorrow night around seven, because you told me you go to bed early during the week. Then we can talk about getting together for dinner at this Italian restaurant I love, because you mentioned you love Italian food. Good food, good conversation, no strings attached."

You've built a "yes" bridge. You've stated your intentions, led her down a road of positivity, and painted a positive scenario—instead of letting her mind dwell on negative possibilities.

Mack Fact: A married man is four times more likely to die during sex if his partner isn't his wife.

8

The Ex Factor

Some women have an unfortunate tendency to talk at length about their prior relationships, especially the ones that ended badly. While this is not a topic you should allow her to dwell on, you need to know how to deal with it if it comes up.

While you want to be sympathetic and attentive, you can only be her shoulder to cry on up to a certain point. You want her to focus on future possibilities with you, not wreckage from the past.

Allow her to have this conversation with you once, and only once. If she wants to vent about her ex on this one occasion, it can strengthen the bond between the two of you and provide you with valuable intel. But if she tries to discuss it the next time you see her or speak on the phone, change the subject: "I understand you went through some difficult times, but I think we should live our lives in the present, not in the past. Right now I'm just thinking about you and me."

Allowing her to discuss her ex (or exes) can work to your advantage in a number of ways:

1. It shows you which types of men she falls for, and which types she has formed strong

negative feelings toward. This is valuable
intel.
2. By knowing what kind of guy burned her
in the past, you can present yourself as the
opposite.
3. You can find out how recently she's been in a
relationship. If it broke off last week, be aware
that she might get back with him. Christopher
learned from his police work that the average
abused woman leaves a relationship *seven times*
before she quits it for good.
4. It shows that you're not insecure talking
about other guys.
5. It shows that you're a good listener.

Remember what we said earlier about how hostage negotiators downplay the word "gun." While conversing about her
ex, never refer to him by name. Refer to him as "that guy."
This diminishes his importance and makes him seem irrele-
vant to what's going on right here and now.

Also, no matter how much of a creep he sounds like, don't
say disparaging things about him. She cared about him
deeply at one time. Saying that he sounds like a loser might
cause her to suddenly get defensive; she gave the guy a piece
of her heart, so in a sense you're insulting her, too. Any critical comments you make about her ex should refer to his *behavior*, not him as a person.

Ex Ranking

Most "exes" fall under one of the following categories:

The Stalker

If the guy couldn't take a hint and kept harassing her after the breakup, you've got to be extra careful about showing *any* potential stalker tendencies. She's on high alert for those red flags.

Paint yourself as the opposite. If her ex got jealous when other guys talked to her, you can say, "I didn't mind when guys would compliment my ex-girlfriend, as long as they were respectful." Plant seeds in her mind; if she were to date you, you would never behave the way *he* did.

Stalkers are incredibly insecure. They smother their girlfriends for fear of losing them to another man. Plant another seed by mentioning to her, "When I'm in a relationship with a girl it's important to spend time together, but I also enjoy my personal space and time to myself."

If this encounter is happening at a nightclub or bar, play it totally cool if she wants to excuse herself to go the bathroom or go talk to some friends. Don't try to go with her. Always give her space. When she returns to you, make a joke: "You came back. I guess I must be doing something right." You are the *opposite* of that guy who shadowed her everywhere she went.

If she makes a comment about how some other guy is checking her out, or tried to mack her on her way back from the bathroom, react in the opposite way that her ex would. Make light of it. Say, "Obviously someone else recognized how pretty you are."

If you wind up exchanging phone numbers with her, maintain this laid-back attitude; assume that her ex probably called her cell phone twenty times a day (he *still* might). Don't sound like you're in a rush to make plans to see her again. You're still going to guide her toward a date and your desired outcome—we'll show you how in our "Phone Control" chapter—but it's important to make her feel that you're in no hurry.

The Cheater

This is another common ex-boyfriend scenario: the guy who was unfaithful. This affects women deeply and damages their trust in all men. One way to overcome this barrier is to drop little "fidelity bombs" throughout the conversation, underscoring how much you value commitment. A good one is, "I love seeing old couples that look like they've been married for fifty years and are still in love. I hope to find a partner like that." If you happen to know a couple that fits this bill, perhaps your parents or grandparents, use them as an example.

Another gem: "One movie that really stuck with me is *Bonnie and Clyde*. No matter what, right up until the very end, they had each other's backs."

This is also a good time to drop the "Cops at the Door" hypothetical. If she stayed loyal to a guy who ran around with other girls, she'll probably answer that hypothetical by saying she'd cover for a guy in that situation. At that point, you underscore how much you also value loyalty. You can add a twist to distance yourself from her ex: "But I also believe loyalty is something you have to *earn*. When I'm in a relationship with someone, I'm very loyal to them, but I expect the same in return."

The hostage negotiator technique to use here with women who've been cheated on is to become her fellow traveler. "I was in a relationship where I was cheated on," you can say. "A lot of people have been there. I remember how I used to beat myself up over it, until I realized it had nothing to do with me and everything to do with them. You're a great person and *he* missed out on a lot." After dropping this gem, you've pretty much said all there is to say on the subject. Move the conversation to another topic, something light and humorous.

The Loser

If her ex was a deadbeat, drop gems that establish you as a responsible, upwardly mobile person. This doesn't mean you should mention the expensive car you drive, or how much money you make. That just sounds like bragging. Do it in a subtler way by talking about the importance of *punctuality*. As you listen to her tales of woe about how her ex was always broke, mooched off of her, etc., say, "It sounds like he wasted a lot your time." Go into a brief riff on punctuality, which is one of the most obvious signs of a man who has his act together. Tell her a quick story about someone who showed up late for an appointment with you. It could have been a business meeting or a date with a woman. "I think everyone's time is valuable," you tell her. "When that person showed up a half hour late, I felt like they didn't respect me and the fact that my time is valuable, too." You've just planted a major seed. You're the polar opposite of a guy who's unorganized and lazy.

The Commitaphobe

If her ex was gunshy about committing to a serious relationship or marrying her, a Mack needs to find this out as soon as possible. The commitaphobe can do more damage to a woman than any other type of ex-boyfriend. When women break up with stalkers, cheaters, or losers, it's for clear-cut reasons. Even if she still has feelings for the guy, she can justify the breakup to herself and to her friends.

Commitaphobes can wreak havoc on a woman's self-esteem because there isn't the same sense of closure. She probably went through a phase where she blamed herself for his refusal to commit: "What is it about *me* that makes him want to date other girls?" Meanwhile, her friends have serious boyfriends and are getting married left and right, which compounds her sense of confusion and frustration.

When you meet a woman whose prior boyfriend was a commitaphobe, plant seeds that show you respect and value commitment. Pepper the conversation with things you have committed to in your life. When talking about jobs, you might emphasize how you're very *committed* to your career or your company. You might be *committed* to staying in good shape, or to achieving a personal goal. If you haven't made any major life commitments yet, perhaps you've been committed to a sports team through the years. Don't bore her with stories about the Boston Red Sox; just mention that you've always stood by your team through thick and thin, and you think that's an important attitude to have in life.

A fun question you might ask is, "Are you a dog person or a cat person?" (If you're highly allergic to cats, this is also intel you ought to know before going back to her place.) Women tend to love animals—some even carry around pet photos in their wallets, to show them off like proud mothers—and dogs and cats cling to their owners. Tell her you love how animals commit to their owners unconditionally.

You never want to come right out and tell her you want to commit to *her*. This makes your intentions obvious, and it might scare her off if she hasn't known you long and wants to take things in steps. But do reinforce in her mind that you have the *potential* to be a committed boyfriend. Men don't tend to consider potential; they judge a woman by what's in front of their face. Women are often willing to view men as works-in-progress. If she feels a guy has the potential to become a good boyfriend or husband, she's usually willing to give it a shot. Unfortunately, some women stay in relationships long after it becomes obvious that he's a commitaphobe and is never going to be the person she hoped he would be.

Protect Your Past

Though you're willing to listen (to a point) about her exes, the rule of thumb is that you should never go into details about your own. Talking about your prior relationships is like stumbling through a minefield. She'll ask why you broke up with your ex (women *always* want to know this), and no matter how it ended it's usually difficult to explain without setting off red flags. Regardless of who dumped whom, or who got caught cheating, or whether you and your ex "just grew apart," the failure of your past relationship only makes her mind generate suspicions about you. It's a road you don't want to go down.

If she inquires about your romantic past, say, "I could tell you some stories, too, but you know what? That was in the past, and this is now. I'd rather focus on you."

There are many other types of exes. Not all are negative; her relationship with him might have simply run its course and there aren't any hard feelings. In that case, note what it was about that guy that attracted her to him, but don't try to "ride his coattails" and drop gems about how you're similar to him. Present yourself as a fresh, original alternative—not only to her ex, but to every guy that she has encountered before.

Advanced Mack Maneuver: Ex Marks the Spot

Another selected entry from Christopher's Mack Journal on www.macktactics.com.

An essential tactic in your road to success is knowing how to utilize your exes. We define an ex as any female who you've ever been with romantically, even if it was just for one night.

For most guys, the thought of being around an ex is awkward and uncomfortable. They'll practically hide under the table if a girl they hooked up with in the past walks into the club. But if you play it smart, exes can be one of the most powerful weapons in your arsenal. You've already spent time, money, and effort on them. Why chuck all that away, when you can keep them as a companion on the nightlife scene? Used correctly, a female "wingman" can be much more effective than a male one.

Make an effort to stay on good terms with the women you've been with. A weekly phone call, just to say hello, goes a long way. When you go out to a club or a bar to mack, you possess a great tactical advantage if you're accompanied by at least one attractive female. It makes other females notice you. They instinctively become curious. Clearly, you've got qualities that make women want to be around you.

Obviously if you dated a girl on a serious basis and broke up, she's not going to enjoy accompanying you on your macking excursions. There's going to be jealousy if she sees you chatting up other women. The trick is to cultivate at least two or three exes with whom you've had "no strings attached" relationships. This works both ways, since women enjoy going out partying with cool male friends. It makes them feel more secure. A male friend can act as a "buffer" between her and the Wolves who want to approach her. Hanging out with an ex can be a win-win situation.

So here's a story to illustrate this principle. My boy Rob and I hit a club on the Vegas Strip. Saturday night, two single guys, well dressed, with plenty of cash on hand. Ready for action . . . or so it might seem.

But here's the ugly truth: most women look at a couple of guys arriving at the club with each other as less-than-attractive options. They know you're lacking female companionship and are anxious to find some. This in itself is a red flag.

This is where the ex-factor came into play. First, understand there are several levels of exes. The most beneficial are the ones who have no serious intentions of having you as a boyfriend. Earlier in the evening I'd called Cathy, a cute twenty-two-year-old cocktail waitress who I had a short-lived fling with back in the day. Aside from the occasional phone call every couple of weeks, we rarely hang out. But I make sure to maintain my relationship with her for nights like these. I told Cathy that me and my boy are rolling out tonight. No strings, no pressure, just good music and good times. And I tell her to invite a friend.

Cathy and her friend are in. Now you're wondering, why did I invite them when we're about to hit a club full of women? Because they're one of the keys to our success tonight. When Rob and I walk into the club and meet up with them, we're a group instead of two desperate-looking guys on the prowl. Never forget: when you show up with a female—or even better, multiple females—the other girls in the place are assessing you. They're wondering what you've got that makes women want to hang with you. Even if your ex isn't the hottest thing on the block, it gives you instant cred with the other girls. It also gives you an element of intrigue.

We sit down and have drinks. Since the four of us came as "friends," I'm under no obligation to pay for drinks, so we take turns buying rounds. Meanwhile, Rob and I are scanning the room, and not five minutes after we sit down, a crew of five model-quality hammers—accompanied by a couple of guys—sit at the table next to ours.

As we sit at our table and laugh and joke, I notice that the hammer crew is checking us out. They notice that my friends and I are getting loose and having fun. Which we are, but at the same time, I'm applying a Mack commandment: "Wherever you're at is the place to be." In other words, my table is where the party is at.

During this, I make eye contact with one of the hammers. I picked out the one that I wanted, a blonde, and waited for our eyes to meet. She's the one on the end, wearing the short denim skirt; she let her eyes linger on me after she took a pull off her smoke, and right then I knew there was mutual interest.

At this point, I'm making Mack mental notes. In the Marine Corps, before any mission you get intel. Macking is no different. She's wearing a skirt: this means she's confident. She smokes: she's got a "bad girl" streak. She sits on the end: independent and looking for more fun than her crew can provide. She drinks out of a martini glass: classy. With this intel, I'm able to formulate the proper strategy for when I eventually get one-on-one with her.

I grab my friend Cathy and take her to the dance floor, and we dance like we're the only two people in the room. Since we were intimate together in the past, we're at ease with each other physically. I know the blonde hammer is checking us out.

After we finish, I walk Cathy back to our table. Now it's time to put in work. When the cocktail waitress returns, I send a drink over to the blonde hammer with specific instructions. I tell the waitress to relay the message that I'm here with a group of *friends* and I like her style, so "enjoy this drink with no strings attached."

Fellas, I could have put my Mack check in the bank right then.

When the waitress brings over the drink and whispers in the hammer's ear, she gives me a smile. I can tell she's flattered and impressed by my gesture.

I give her a friendly smile and go back to chatting with my group, like I have all the time in the world. Of course, I know it's only a matter of time before I wind up standing next to the blonde hammer on the dance floor, or at the bar. When we do wind up talking (I time it so I "encounter" her in the hallway outside the bathrooms), the ice is already broken. I know which subjects to hit during our conversation, based on my observations about her, and it's easy to get her digits and set a date for later in the week.

Show up alone, or with a guy, and girls will rarely notice you; you have to work twice as hard to make them interested in you. Show up with girls—preferably an ex and her friend(s)—and you are noticed immediately, and have a powerful tactical advantage.

9

Target-Rich Environments

After dark is when most guys attempt to meet women, with nightclubs and bars being the most obvious pickup environments. (For many men, these are the *only* environments where they'll attempt to mack since it allows them to gulp down some "liquid courage.")

While the hot clubs in your town may be hammer magnets, they can also be challenging environments. Competition is in the air. Other guys, who we call Wolves, are everywhere, all competing for the same women. Beyond the testosterone overload, you've got to deal with other factors such as smoke, loud music, and the money you've got to spend on drinks.

But the toughest obstacle you face in a nightclub is the attitude women adopt in these environments. They're on guard, like airport metal detectors on high alert. Sometimes it's difficult to initiate a casual, innocent-sounding conversation, because in this environment women automatically assume that you're hitting on them. On top of this, she's probably there with friends—who tend to interrupt (especially the jealous unattractive ones), and may drag her away to the bathroom just when you're starting to make progress.

Using M.A.C.K. Tactics, you can certainly succeed with women in nightclubs, but when it comes to picking target-rich environments you need to think beyond the obvious "meat markets." Remember Mack commandment 6: "Be original." This extends to the places where you go to meet new women.

A Mack we know, while driving in his car, picked up on the fact that billboards for real-estate agents are all over his town, and in supermarkets and 7-Elevens there were free real-estate magazines filled with ads for more agents. In these ads, the agent is pictured and the majority of them were females. Some are quite classy-looking and attractive. So he called a pretty one and told her he wanted to see a certain home that she was handling the sale for. She was glad to meet him and give him a personal tour. (She wasn't married; he looked out for telltale signs, like a wedding ring in her picture or a hyphenated last name.)

As a Mack, he knew this was about more than getting to know the real-estate agent. Although he wasn't looking to purchase a house—the one he toured was beyond his price range—it expanded his knowledge of houses, home decoration, and the real-estate market. (Remember that becoming a successful Mack means constantly acquiring new knowledge.) He also was impressed by the agent's sales skills and even learned some new conversational moves. He realized that good salespeople are like Macks, able to quickly establish connections with people, become their ally and gain their trust, and guide them toward "yes" answers.

Christopher has done the same thing while car shopping. Car lots tend to have attractive women on staff; ignore the overzealous salesmen and let a female show you some vehicles. All you need is a valid driver's license and you can take a spin in any car on the lot, with her riding shotgun. Though Christopher rarely made a purchase, he usually went home with a salesgirl's phone number and learned about a cool new ride to boot.

If you drive a crappy car, spending some time on car lots serves a purpose the next time a woman asks you what kind of car you drive. Use the principle of articulate avoidance: instead of admitting that you drive an '87 Dodge Dart, tell her about that Lexus or Hummer you took for a test drive the other day. This way, instead of admitting one of your vulnerable areas, you're implying that you're an ambitious guy who appreciates luxury vehicles and is interested in buying one. (You might be a few years from being able to afford one, but she doesn't need to know that detail.)

Our friend who toured the expensive house could use the same form of articulate avoidance when asked about where he lives. Instead of telling the girl about the apartment he shares with his roommate, he could talk about his helpful real-estate agent and the luxury homes he's been checking out. Nothing he was saying was untrue.

> *One important note: unless you're seriously thinking about buying a home or car, don't allow them to run your credit. It lowers your credit score.*

We're not saying you need to start touring homes and hanging around car lots. The point is that there target-rich environments around you that you've been overlooking. We've already discussed how the saleswomen at your local mall can be a great asset. Spend a couple of hours leisurely browsing at the mall; you can chat up all kinds of hammers while learning about new colognes, women's perfumes, jewelry, and clothes. You'll rack up tons of free advice on how to enhance your appearance from a female's perspective.

Try taking a class or joining an activity group in your spare time. If you're interested in women from a certain part of the world, take a language class. Before you sign up and pay, ask to sit in on one of the classes and check out the ratio of men to women. You can mack on women from your class, and go to clubs and restaurants to test out your new skills on women who speak that language. Foreign women are flattered when an American guy makes that type of effort to learn about their language and culture.

Pet stores and animal shelters are other original environments. The women who are working and browsing in these places have their guard down around all those cute little puppies and kittens. Bookstores, coffee shops, the library, the gym, the supermarket . . . anywhere you go where there are single women, you can start casual conversations. Just note her body language before you approach. If she looks stressed out or preoccupied, leave her alone and let her do her thing. You never want to be intrusive.

When initiating conversations with women in these various environments, you'll want to use the three-point intro we explained in the "Conversation Control" chapter: notice her (and have her notice you), then approach, offer your hand, and introduce yourself by name. To give it a more natural flow, it often helps to lead off with a prefacing statement or question based on the environment you are in.

Here are some examples of things you might say in certain environments. As you continue taking "batting practice" and introducing yourself to various women, you'll come up with your own. Whenever the woman responds in a friendly manner, introduce yourself and go from there. Note that asking a woman for some advice is often a good way to go.

Girl in bookstore. Note the book she's looking at. Ask her if she's read other books by that author, or on that subject, i.e., "I've been meaning to pick up some books on psychology. I've always found that topic really interesting." You might add, "I took a course on it in college."

Girl in clothing store. If she's browsing in the men's section, don't bother (unless she makes friendly eye contact with you); she's probably shopping for her husband or boyfriend. If she's shopping in the women's section, pick out a female clothing item and say, "Excuse me, could I ask your opinion on something?" If she's okay with that, show her the item and explain that you're shopping for a gift for a friend. What does she think? Does she have any other suggestions? You can throw in, "I like the way you dress, I thought you'd be a good person to ask."

Girl in grocery store. Take an item off the shelf that you don't know how to prepare and ask her if she has ever tried it. Is it easy to make? How does it taste?

Original environments are a means of meeting women in a way that feels natural and casual. For you *and* her, it can be a more comfortable situation than trying to spark up a conversation in a bar. The deeper effect is that exploring these environments will make you a more worldly and interesting person. Just imagine how pleasantly surprised women will be when they call and ask what you're up to tonight, and you say you've got poetry class, that you're learning a new language, or that on Wednesday nights you volunteer at the youth center. If you're constantly developing and improving yourself, you lead a life that women will want to be a part of.

Advanced Mack Maneuver: The Walk Away

In a busy bar or nightclub, the attractive woman never has any shortage of suitors. She *expects* men to jump at the opportunity to buy her a drink and talk to her. She's essentially giving them the chance to "audition" for her, a role the average guy eagerly accepts.

In this type of environment, the advanced Mack may take an opposite approach. Instead of trying to engage her in a conversation right off the bat, he'll introduce himself, get a positive reaction, then excuse himself and walk away. This knocks her for a loop and leaves her wondering. It also sets the stage for a second encounter later in the evening.

Christopher uses this tactic all the time. As he passes by a girl, he'll make a quick intro and pay her a compliment on her fashion sense: "Hello, my name is Christopher. I just wanted to tell you, I love that outfit you've got on. You've got great style."

When she says, "Thank you," she's expecting him to initiate a conversation or offer to buy her a drink. Instead, he says, "You have a good time tonight. Don't do anything I wouldn't do." He then gives her a smile and walks away.

The girl is flattered—and a little bit confused. Now *there's* a confident guy, she thinks; he paid her a compliment, captured her interest, then went back to doing his own thing. Obviously this is not a guy who is lacking for female company.

But Christopher intends to encounter her again. Perhaps an hour later he sees her going to the ladies' room and moves to that area of the club so that he can catch her eye as she comes out. Then he references their earlier encounter: "Hey, it's the best-dressed girl in the club."

This time, instead of walking away, he starts conversing with her. The ice has already been broken; he has established that he's not eager to "pick her up." At this point, she might even feel flattered that he's taking the time to talk to her. After all, this is a guy who must have other options.

Sometimes Christopher will drop this funny little gem, delivered with a smile: "I wasn't trying to pick you up before, but I am now. Let's go get a drink."

You can't put a price tag on a line like that.

10

Women to Be Wary Of

When you meet a girl for the first time, you're not meeting the real her. You're meeting her representative, the image she is trying to project. Women put up fronts for any number of reasons (just as men do), whether it's vanity, insecurity, shyness, or the fact they don't want to reveal their attraction to you. Using conversation-control techniques (such as hypotheticals) is how you get them to open up and reveal their true nature.

As a Mack, you want to cut through the facade and get to know "the real her" as soon as possible. Before you invest a significant amount of time in her, you must determine whether she's going to be worth your efforts. The Mack doesn't hesitate to make a polite exit if he knows he's not going to mesh with a particular woman. You must maintain the attitude that your options are limitless. For Macks, they truly are.

In this chapter, we'll identify certain categories of problematic women. Each gives off warning signals, or "red flags," that you need to be able to pick up on. Just because a woman falls under one of the following categories doesn't mean you should forget about her. Some of these women may be fine for one-night stands or casual relationships, or as a friend to accompany you when you go out. But definitely think twice before making any type of commitment.

It should be noted that everyone has the capacity for change, and a skilled Mack can often mold a woman over time to fit his groove. It's up to you whether you want to devote effort to a "work in progress." As a rule of thumb, however, beginning Macks should avoid the following categories and focus on meeting women who are less likely to create problems.

The money chick. The signals are usually clear: the designer outfits, the jewelry, the hot (often surgically enhanced) body she loves to show off. She acts like she's above every guy in the room, but wants to be the center of attention.

The money chick wants men who will treat her to the finer things. If you're not prepared to drop serious loot, she's not interested. Even if you do write her the proverbial "blank check," she might still entertain offers from other guys who are down to spend cash on her. As long as she looks as good as she does, there will never be any shortage of guys willing to do so.

But never *assume* she's a money chick just because of her appearance. A lot of guys have convinced themselves that hot women are only interested in rich guys. This gives them an excuse not to approach these women and risk rejection. With extremely attractive women, the key is to project confidence—not cockiness, but an attitude that says "I might be interested in knowing you better, but I'm not impressed yet." As we've stated before, never comment on her looks. She gets those compliments from the Wack Pack all day long. It's the most predictable thing you could say.

If you suspect she might be a money chick, you'll want to either confirm or disprove those suspicions. Here, conversation control is especially important. In order to capture her interest, you must distinguish yourself from the Wack Pack by engaging her with thoughtful questions and topics. Meanwhile, always remember Mack commandment 8: "three-quarters of macking is listening." The more she talks about herself, the easier it will be to learn her true nature.

You can bust out special hypotheticals to test the waters. Tell her a story along these lines:

> *You* (as you check your cell phone): "I'm just seeing if my friend Mike called. He was really bummed out today."
> *Her:* "Why?"
> *You:* "He had a date last night with a girl. But when he showed up at her house to take her to dinner, she took one look at the car he was driving and said, 'On second thought, maybe this isn't such a good idea.' She dissed him because he drives a beat-up car."

Chuckle while you tell the story, then see how she responds. You can follow up with, "Would you ever not date a guy because of his car?" If she displays an arrogant attitude ("I don't date broke guys" or "I'm not going to be seen driving around in some crappy car"), then it's safe to say you're dealing with a money chick.

Another hypothetical: "My buddy Mike just got back from a trip to New York. He bought a fake Cartier watch off some street vendor for twenty dollars. He gave it to his girlfriend as a gift. She's thrilled, thinking he gave her this superexpensive watch. Now he feels bad about it and wants to tell her it's a fake, but he doesn't want to disappoint her."

Again, tell it as a humorous story. Note her reaction. Is she disgusted by the idea of a man giving a woman a fake watch? Does she make a comment about how *she* could tell the difference between a Cartier and a fake? Or does she show a less materialistic attitude, saying something to the effect of, "I guess as long as it makes her happy . . ." You might be surprised at how genuine and down-to-earth she actually is. A lot of beautiful women are much sweeter than you might think.

The Mack is never intimidated by money chicks, but respects their game. These girls are players in their own right and know how to wrap men around their manicured fingers. Generally they'll respect you, too, if you project confidence and seem difficult to impress. That's not a vibe they're used to getting from men.

Then again, maybe you've got big bucks and are looking to bag yourself the hottest trophy on the block. Some guys have the finances to play the money chick's game and like having a woman on their arm that most men can only fantasize about. If so, more power to you. Just know what you're getting into and don't spend more than you can afford.

One-night-stand chick. She's a bad girl and wants you to know it. She makes sexual references even though she just met you. She makes frequent physical contact: touching you, brushing up against you, grinding on the dance floor. It seems like she's good to go, but if you don't seal the deal with her tonight, some other guy will. With girls like these, you rarely get a second chance.

If you're down for this type of action, it's all about seizing the moment. Isolate her by bringing her to an area of the club or bar where you can hang out away from the crowd. Don't sit there making out with her endlessly. Make your exit with her and take the party back to your place. The longer you stick around, the greater the chance that some other guy is going to screw things up for you.

These girls get off on being shocking. The key is to never be timid and to give as good as you get. Tease her a little and make her prove just how much of a bad girl she is. If she likes talking about sex, smile and say, "You talk a good game, but I don't know if you can back it up." As a Mack, you shouldn't get into raunchy sex talk. But this is a good time to drop the "voyeur" hypothetical. It will keep the conversation frisky, at a PG-13 level. Things will get R-, and hopefully X-rated, once you're alone with her.

Rebound chick. This type of female is still bruised from a relationship gone bad. Maybe the breakup occurred a week ago; maybe it happened years ago and she still can't get over the guy. In any event, you're dealing with wreckage that another man left behind. Refer to the "Ex Factor" chapter for specific techniques on how to set her mind straight and refocus it on you.

Just remember to be cautious. Listen sympathetically while gathering intel. But once she's told you the whole sad story, end that topic of discussion. The longer you let her go on about her romantic problems, the more she'll begin to view you as a "good friend" rather than a romantic partner. Once she mentally places you in that "friend box," that's where you will remain.

Drama queens, man haters, and consumers. You never want to get emotionally attached to these types of females. They might be okay for a short fling, but be aware that you're playing with fire. Dating these women on a serious level will only create turmoil in your life.

To the drama queen, every minor problem is a crisis. Her problems become your headaches. She has a complaint about everything and thinks everyone is trying to screw her over or stab her in the back—but nothing is ever *her* fault. She pays little attention to anyone else's problems, including yours, but wants everyone to know about hers.

Christopher has a rule of thumb: if he hears three different complaints from a woman within ten minutes of meeting her, he tags her as a drama queen and walks in the other direction. There's a big difference between being a sympathetic listener and letting a woman unload her problems on you, especially if she barely knows you. This type of personality is extremely difficult to deal with long-term. There will always be something new for her to complain about.

Man haters are females who have been mistreated by men throughout their lives, probably beginning with their father. During the course of your conversation, she makes statements like, "All men are dogs," or, "Guys only care about one thing." She has serious issues with men and does not trust them.

Don't argue with the man hater or try to convince her otherwise. And forget about trying to make moves on her, since this will only confirm her beliefs.

So how should you handle it? *M.A.C.K. Tactics* takes a unique approach with man haters. As a Mack, you can turn this negative situation into a positive by using the concept of "Pay It Forward" (as in the Kevin Spacey film of that name). Ask her why she feels the way she does. Don't mack on her; just listen, converse with her on a friendly level, and do none of the things she expects "all men" to do. Agree with her, at least partially: "I understand what you mean. Unfortunately, there *are* a lot of men out there like the ones you're describing."

This is not a waste of your time. By doing this, you are demonstrating to her that there *are* decent guys out there; she's talking to one. In effect, you're acting as a wingman for the entire male brotherhood. After chatting for a little while and hearing her out, tell her that you really enjoyed meeting her and politely excuse yourself. The mere fact that you didn't try to get anything from her (a phone number, a date, etc.) will force her to reevaluate her feelings. It may not change her mind about men, but a seed has been planted— and because of it, the next guy down the road might have some success with her.

Pay it forward—the good karma that a Mack puts out inevitably returns to him.

Consumers are females who are always asking for things but don't reciprocate. They're almost like low-budget money chicks, the difference being that money chicks go for much bigger scores (they want the diamonds, not the free lunch).

Here are some examples of typical consumer behavior.

- **She asks you to buy her a drink before you offer it.**
- **She needs to use your cell phone—multiple times in one evening.**
- **She bums rides off you, sometimes asking you to drive significant distances.**
- **In the car, she asks you to stop for things (i.e., alcohol, food), then expects you to pay for it.**
- **When a bill arrives, she never even pretends to make an effort to chip in.**
- **She's excited to see you or talk to you on the phone when she needs something. Otherwise, she's usually in a bad mood or stressed out.**
- **She calls you to talk about her problems, but doesn't inquire about the things going on in *your* life.**

When the consumer says "thanks," there's usually no real gratitude behind it. She expects these things, probably because she dates weak men who tolerate this behavior. A lot of men are willing to fork over the cash because they don't want to look cheap. But the Mack knows that has nothing to do with it. It's about respect. Making constant demands on your time and wallet is a form of disrespect that the Mack does not tolerate.

We avoid consumers, but in the time we've spent hanging out on the Vegas club scene we've met enough of them to fill a whole separate book. These women always have money to get their hair done and buy new outfits, yet they bum rides because they don't have a car. They flirt with guys just long enough to get free drinks. They borrow money from friends and always have a sob story why they can't pay them back. They figure their looks give them a "free pass."

There are different levels of consumers. In the extreme cases that we've given, they're vacuums that suck up the time, money, and energy of everyone around them. But a consumer can also be subtle and crafty. It's not about the size of her requests; it's about a consistent pattern of behavior. *She always needs something.*

You can perform little "tests" to see if she has consumer tendencies:

• **You're talking to her at a bar. You say that you need a napkin. Note her reflex response. Does** she check to see if there's a napkin nearby to hand you, or does she let you figure it out?

• You're having drinks with her. You've been paying for the rounds so far; now it's time to order the next one. You check your wallet and mention that you're almost out of cash. Does she reach into her purse and offer to pay for the next round, or does she just sit there and wait for you to go find an ATM?

You can learn a lot about a woman's nature by noting the way she reacts to *your* little requests. If she's a "subtle consumer," she might be worth putting up with for the time being. But unless you are able to correct her behavior, her consumer mentality will become very annoying in an ongoing relationship. This is because as a Mack, you're aware of it; most guys aren't able to recognize that red flag.

Christopher tells a story to illustrate. We'll call this . . .

Advanced Mack Maneuver: Cutting Off the Consumer

A while back I was in San Diego at a bar by the beach. I was macking this girl named Samantha, and she was macking me. I could tell she had game. I wasn't picking up on any red flags, but then things took a turn.

When the bartender came over, I ordered a beer for myself, and Samantha told the bartender she wanted a margarita. I hadn't asked her if she wanted anything, but when the check came she didn't flinch. She assumed that I would pay for the round. Then she asked to bum a cigarette. A few minutes later she asked me to order an appetizer from the bar, so we could "share it."

After we finished eating, she asked if we could drive to a party. She said it was "close," but I knew from the address that it was on the other side of town. We left the bar together and hopped in my car. When I turned on the radio, she changed the station without asking. Then I stopped to buy some gas. While I was filling up the tank, she asked me to go inside and buy some beer so we'd have something to drink in case the party was running low. She also asked me to buy some gum for her.

What happened next came as a surprise to her. Instead of heading into the 7-Eleven, I got back in the car and said that I'd changed my mind; I wasn't in the mood to go to a party. I politely explained that I was feeling tired and had work in the morning, but I would give her a ride to the party if she wanted.

So I drove her to the party. Before she got out of the car, we kissed for a while and she gave me her phone number (which I won't be calling).

I didn't go home. I hit a club instead and put in a different kind of "work." The next day I thought about the time I'd spent with Samantha and how I should have recognized her red flags even sooner.

The things she asked for were minor. I wasn't concerned about the cost of some drinks, gas, or a pack of gum. She always asked in a sweet way, and she said her "thank-yous." It was the pattern of behavior that bothered me. She was constantly asking me for something—a guy she barely knew. She was a cool girl, but she was also a consumer. And that's a game I don't play.

Mack Fact: The first episode of *Joanie Loves Chachi* was the highest-rated American program in the history of Korean television. Maybe this was because "Chachi" is the Korean word for "penis."

11

Phone Control

I was ordering dessert when they were eating dinner.
When they were having coffee, I was asking for a check.
I had business.
—*Ray Liotta*, GoodFellas

A Mafia boss once said that every time he put a phone to his ear, he treated it like he had a gun to his head. He never knew when the Feds were listening in. If he carelessly mentioned a name or referred to a certain piece of "business," it could bring down his whole empire.

As a Mack, you need to approach phone calls with women the same way.

After exchanging numbers with a woman, the biggest question for most guys is how long they should wait before calling her. They worry that if they call the next day, they'll appear desperate, but if they wait a day or two the girl might forget about them.

Here's the simple answer. If you used conversation control during your initial meeting with her, don't worry. She *will* remember you. You established yourself as a fun, original individual. At the same time, you were a good listener.

She probably told you things about herself that she wouldn't tell the average guy. If you laid this groundwork the first time you met her, she'll be looking forward to talking to you on the phone. There's no need for you to feel awkward or anxious about it. The door is wide open.

She also remembers you as a confident guy. Confident men take action; those words are two of the Pillars of Power in the word M.A.C.K. So if you want to see her again and she doesn't call you by 7 P.M. the following evening, pick up the phone and give her a ring.

You've got absolutely nothing to lose. You're a train moving full steam ahead. With or without her, you're going to keep macking and making moves. You're giving her the *opportunity* to take a ride with you.

When You Call Her

The key is to call her *with a purpose*. If your goal is to set up a date, have a plan mapped out before you pick up the phone. When you met her, you should have learned what her schedule is like. Does she work nights? Is she free on the weekends? Does she enjoy going out for drinks or coffee at a particular place? Is she a night owl or does she prefer daytime activities?

If you applied proper conversation control, you already know the answers to these questions before you make the phone call. You're now going to chat, get to know her a little more, and then suggest a time and a place to get together that should work for her.

If she doesn't answer, never hang up. Always leave a message. Assume she has caller ID; you don't want it to look like you chickened out. Then, when you leave the message, sound energized and confident: "Hi, Michelle, this is John.

We met a couple of nights ago. I'm going to a couple of interesting things later in the week that I wanted to let you know about. Give me a call back, 867-5309."

What are the "interesting things" you are referring to? It's the place, or places, that you were planning on inviting her to for your first date. (We'll explain in a moment why it's important to *extend invitations*, rather than asking her out in the conventional way.)

If she answers, view this first phone conversation with her as a "mini date." You're not calling her to engage in random chitchat. You are executing a plan.

Don't ask, "Have I caught you at a bad time?" or "Can you talk?" This sounds apologetic. Assume that she's been waiting for your call. If it's not a good time for her to talk, she'll let you know.

Keep the conversation light. Ask her simple questions that prompt her to talk: "How's your day been going?" Keep your responses brief and don't volunteer any information about yourself that she doesn't already know. Wait until you see her again to get more in-depth.

Another hostage negotiation technique to use in this scenario: the negotiator will remind the hostage taker of things he said in order to show that he was listening. This strengthens their bond. ("I remember you mentioned you had a daughter. How old is she?" or "I remember you said you were hungry. I can see about helping you with that.")

On the phone with her, you can say, "I remember you said you worked at the mall. Was it busy today?" or "You mentioned you were looking for an apartment. Have you made any progress with that?" It's a way to keep the conversation flowing, while showing that you were listening to the things she said. Most guys have a terrible memory when it comes to these little details.

After chatting for a short period (five minutes or less), it's time to arrange plans with her. You're going to use the intel you have gathered to suggest a specific time and place to meet. *This will be an invitation to join you for an activity that you already had "planned."*

> **Wack Tactic:** "So maybe one of these nights when you're not busy, we could do something."
> **Mack Tactic:** "So Michelle, I remember you said you were off on Saturdays and you like Italian food. I've been meaning to check out this Italian restaurant I've heard great things about. Why don't we go together?"
> **Wack Tactic:** "If you don't have plans Saturday night, I was thinking we could have dinner."
> **Mack Tactic:** "I'm going to check out this cool jazz café on Thursday night. I remember you said that's your night off and you love jazz. Why don't we go together?"

Notice the phrasing: you're going to visit this spot with or without her. (It could be an art gallery, a café, the beach—wherever you want to take her on this date.) The message you're sending is that you already have plans in motion and you're extending an offer for her to join you. This approach should give you complete confidence. If she declines for any reason, there's no need for you to feel awkward; you were going to go anyway.

Something else to bear in mind: if you met her in a nightclub or at a party, any environment where it's loud or the alcohol is flowing, you might not be certain this is a woman you *want* to take out on a date. This phone chat is then a

chance for you to feel her out a little more and make that de-
termination. If you weren't able to gather certain bits of important intel—her schedule, her interests, etc.—you can
gain the answers during this phone call. Ideally, however,
you should have gathered this intel when you first met her.

Make all of your phone chats with women concise and
purposeful. Don't hang on the line for too long, and avoid
subjects that require you to go into long explanations. Remember, the Mack always conveys the impression that he
has other things going on in his life. Your phone conversations with her should have a purpose: to set up a date, or to
keep things flowing with her until you have your next date.

If you get another incoming call while you're talking to
her, don't take it. Call the other person back once you've finished conversing with her. Just think about how you feel
when you're speaking with someone, and they say, "Hold on,
I need to take this call." It always feels mildly insulting.

The five-minute limit is flexible. If she has a problem she
needs to talk to you about, then of course it's okay to give her
more of your time. But don't let her go on endlessly. As we all
know, women tend to enjoy chatting on the phone a lot
more than men do. Some women like to have guys as "phone
friends" that they can chat with but don't want to commit to
going out on dates with. Don't let these women waste your
time. If she enjoys talking to you, then she should have no
qualms about meeting you again in person.

Another note on phone etiquette: the outgoing message
on your cell and/or home phone should convey confidence
and be brief. Ask callers to leave their name and end it on a
positive note, i.e., "God bless" or "Take care." Nothing corny,
just a short, positive phrase. And don't play a song in the

background. That might have sounded cool back in high
school. Now, it sounds juvenile.

If She Calls You

If you exchange numbers and she calls you first, it's an excellent
sign. But again, you can't make yourself available for a long
chat. The message you want to send is that you were in the
middle of something, but you're willing to make time for her.

When she asks what you're up to, don't say "nothing." Tell
her you're finishing up some work, getting ready to go out,
cooking dinner—something that suggests you're engaged in
an activity but will put it aside to give her your attention.

When she makes the first call, don't attempt to set up a
date. You don't want her to think you're in a hurry to see her
again, or that you've been waiting for her call to ask her out.
Just chat with her. Once it's been five minutes, tell her you've
got something you need to take care of. Ask her, "When is a
good time for me to call you tomorrow?" You will be prepared to make this call. This is when you will invite her out.

It's important to lock down the specific time when you
will call her. By calling her then, you show that you're punc-
tual and you will avoid having to leave messages and playing
phone tag. Calling a girl and accidentally waking her up, or
someone she lives with, is an awkward situation. You can put
a cute little twist on it by asking, "What's your bedtime? I
wouldn't want to wake you up."

More Phone Fundamentals

When you're out on a date, shut your phone off or keep it on
vibrate. Only wannabe Macks enjoy taking calls when they're

with a woman, in the mistaken belief that it makes them look important. In reality, important people can't be bothered every time someone calls them to chat.

If you absolutely must answer your phone in front of her, be polite and apologetic: "Do you mind if I answer this? It's an important call." Ninety-nine percent of women will say of course, go ahead. Keep the call short and businesslike, then focus your full attention back on her. Make her feel like your priority.

Only take phone calls from women when you're in the right frame of mind to talk. If you're stressed out or in a bad mood, or in an environment that makes it difficult to converse, don't answer. Call her back when you're ready to do so. You will always have the opportunity to speak with her again. It's always better to ignore the call than to give off negative energy or make her feel like she's less important than whatever you're doing at the moment.

If the date you set up with her is more than three days away, call her once more between now and then. The purpose of this phone call is to confirm your plans; you don't want her to forget.

If you begin dating a woman, it's perfectly okay to speak with her on the phone on a daily basis. If you enjoy talking to her every day, great. You can increase the length of your phone chats, but don't always be the one calling her. If you call her two days in a row, end the second call by saying, "Give me a ring tomorrow when you have time," or "Call me tomorrow when you're done with work." Make *her* put forth the effort. It's also a way to gauge her interest level in you.

12

Bad Boy 101

It's a question that has perplexed and tormented the male species since the invention of tattoos: what is it about "bad boys" that mesmerizes women? They shoot down the "nice guys" and hang out with men who are often insensitive and selfish. Oftentimes, the worse bad boys treat them, the more desperately their women cling to them.

Being a bad boy doesn't necessarily mean you are disrespectful to women. It means that you possess an edge, an attitude that says, "I don't *need* anyone—but if you're down to party, let's have some fun." Famous examples of bad boys range from James Dean to Colin Farrell, from Mick Jagger to Tupac. Even without fame and fortune, these guys would be chick magnets. They live (or lived) by their own rules and have an aura of danger, a lifestyle that fascinates men and women alike.

There's a saying that goes, "Women want to marry the guy in the suit, but party with the guy on the Harley." Consider the guys that Princess Diana, one of the classiest and most desirable women in the world, hooked up with after she broke it off with Prince Charles: they included a bodyguard and a jet-setting playboy. Back when Madonna was the hottest sex symbol on the planet, she married hard-drinking, paparazzi-punching Sean Penn. Nicole Kidman, the actress who epitomizes Hollywood glamour, romped with Lenny Kravitz. Pamela Anderson bounced from Tommy Lee (a bad boy supreme, previously married to Heather Locklear) to Kid Rock. J Lo fell for Puff Daddy and wound up dodging gunfire in a nightclub.

Some experts say the attraction is biological, hardwired into the DNA of the female species. Bad boys are hypermasculine. Their veins are coursing with testosterone and they're sexually promiscuous, ready to mate and procreate. They also tend to be egotistical and demand respect. They have a predator mentality, rather than allowing themselves to be preyed upon. This makes them better equipped to survive in a harsh world than men who are soft and overly sensitive. Some women respond to this type of bad boy behavior on a primal level, without even consciously understanding why.

At the bottom of the bad boy barrel are those who are abusive to women, emotionally or physically. The type of women who subject themselves to these relationships are not ones that you, as a Mack, should ever get involved with. These women are emotionally damaged and have horrible self-esteem, despite how physically attractive they might be. Rule them out as options. Don't be foolish enough to think that you can reform or rescue them; they'll cause you nothing but drama and grief, two things no self-respecting Mack is going to put up with.

The film *Casino* contains a perfect example of this: Ginger (Sharon Stone) is a gorgeous prostitute who marries Ace Rothstein (Robert DeNiro), a rich, powerful casino boss. Ace worships the ground she walks on. He showers her with jewelry and furs. He "rescues" her from prostitution, yet she can't break off her relationship with her sleazy former pimp. She turns Ace's life into a living hell, running off with the pimp and taking their child with her. It drives Ace crazy; he can't comprehend why she would choose such a lowlife over him.

Unfortunately, these "fatal attractions" happen all the time. Bad boys can have a powerful grip on psychologically damaged women, and it's a trap that has ruined many other-wise sensible, successful men. Remind yourself that as a Mack, there are an endless number of fun, attractive women out there who will appreciate you. You are squandering your gifts—and even worse, damaging your self-esteem—by at-taching yourself to negative women.

But whether you love them or hate them, there are les-sons to be learned by observing bad boys' behavior. As a Mack you can adopt certain traits of theirs into your game. If you're a good-natured guy, as most of us are, this doesn't mean you need to start treating women poorly. This is about adding an edge to your personality, an infusion of bad boy energy—an aura that says, "I don't *need* anyone, but if you're down to party, let's have some fun."

The following are three key characteristics that bad boys share with Macks:

Bad Boys Don't Wear Their Hearts on Their Sleeves

Over two thousand years ago, the philosopher Aristotle stated, "He who confesses first loses." This principle still ap-plies today, particularly to macking.

To understand this principle, you must first understand the difference between how men and women judge success with the opposite sex. When a man is interested in a woman, he judges success by how much physical contact he makes with her. When a woman is interested in a man, she considers it a success when she confirms he feels the same way about her.

Read that sentence again and think about it. Once you've made it clear to a woman that you like her, you've satisfied her core need. This isn't always a bad thing; if the feeling is mutual, then a relationship can bloom.

But if she's still feeling you out, trying to decide whether she wants to commit to you romantically, you can ruin your chances by jumping the gun and stating how much you like her. Suddenly, she no longer needs to prove anything to you. She knows she can have you if she wants you; you've put the ball in her court. This is the point where many women will lose interest.

Why? Because attractive women get hit on by men every day of their lives. Most of these men wear their emotions on their sleeves, telling them how good-looking they are or trying to ask them out before it's appropriate to do so. Because women have to deal with this on a constant basis, they build up a natural defense mechanism against overanxious men: they instantly rule them out. *When a man confesses his attraction, they tune out.*

Bad boys don't make it so easy. While they're getting to know a girl, they might give her flirtatious looks, a wink, a smile—but like an expert poker player, they don't reveal their true emotions. They keep the woman guessing: *he's flirting, but is he really interested in me?* This will make her want to *keep* playing the game. She'll want to look her best, and act her sexiest in order to get the confirmation she craves. Bad boys can work otherwise sensible women into a frenzy this way.

Never admit to her how long you'd wanted to ask her out, how attracted you are to her, or how you want to be in a committed relationship with her. Although these may sound like romantic gestures, it's more likely that she'll regard it as weakness on your part. Nine times out of ten, your "confession" isn't going to prompt her to confess her own attraction to you. It will only take you down a notch in her eyes. You are no longer an original; you are just another guy who can't control his mouth or his emotions.

Play it cool, be disciplined, and apply M.A.C.K. Tactics. The rest will take care of itself. Remember, you're a train moving full steam ahead. The choice is hers: she can climb onboard, or you can roll without her to the next stop. Either way, you're going to do your thing.

Another advantage of M.A.C.K. Tactics is that if you use the right conversational techniques and "build the bridge," it should become clear whether she is interested in you on a romantic level. Let her be the one to express her feelings to you, and when she does, play it even cooler. Don't commit too early by saying, "You're the only girl I want to be with," or "I want to take this relationship to the next level." Rather, say, "I like spending time with you," or "I enjoy hanging out with you." She'll want to keep earning points with you, to get the confirmation that she desires. *You* are holding the cards.

Bad Boys Lead Their Own Lives

A Mack is a man on the move. He fits women into his schedule, not the other way around. Be fun, charming, and respectful, but don't be easy to pin down. And remember what you learned in the "Phone Control" chapter: in the early stages of a relationship, when she calls you wanting to chitchat, keep the conversation brief.

By doing so, you place yourself in a category she isn't used to dealing with. Most guys will hang on the phone for as long as she wants to talk, even if it means listening to her complain about her ex-boyfriend for an hour. Whenever she's free, these guys will put everything else aside to take her out. If she wants to eat at a fancy restaurant, they gladly pick up the check even if it's beyond their budget.

Inevitably, women grow bored with this type of man. If he's always available, it's a sign that he has nothing else going on his life, and that no other women are interested in him. Women are intrigued by a man who is a "hot commodity," not one who's sitting around waiting to make plans with them.

Instead of immediately accepting her offer the next time she invites you to hang out, create IOUs. When a girl calls a Mack to say, "My friends and I are going to the club, do you want to meet up?" he won't commit right away. Instead, he'll say, "I have some people I need to see, but maybe later I can come by."

He may choose to not show up at all. He'll tell her the next day, "Sorry, something came up." If she's interested in him, this will only increase his allure. The next time they hang out she's going to make an effort to not let him slip through her fingers. If she thinks he has other options, the pressure is on *her* to keep his interest.

You've got an action-packed life to lead. Show her that you're secure in yourself and don't need a woman to complete you.

Bad Boys Are Decisive

The bad boy, like the Mack, doesn't follow the woman's lead. When he goes out for a meal, he knows what he likes to eat. He knows which movie he wants to see. He knows which spots he likes and the types of environments he prefers to be in. And when he arranges a date with a woman, he doesn't ask her opinion on where they should go. He already has the evening mapped out.

Wack Tactic: "So what do you feel like doing?"
Mack Tactic: "I'll pick you up at eight. We're going to do something fun tonight."

Women respect a man who leads. Figure out in advance where you want to take her, so that you never appear hesitant or unsure. A man who can't make up his mind is a man she will quickly lose interest in. Project an air of self-assuredness at all times. As long as you lead, an interested woman will follow.

13

Wingmen

When the character of a man is not clear to you,
look at his friends.
—Japanese proverb

Some say that behind every great man is a great woman. While the accuracy of that statement is questionable (we know plenty of guys who have proven otherwise), we have our own spin on that phrase: "Behind every great Mack is a great wingman."

The term "wingman" derives from military jargon, referring to a fellow fighter pilot who has your back when you fly into combat. In the realm of macking, it means a male friend who accompanies you when you approach women.

The most common wingman scenario is this: you're in a party environment. You want to approach a woman but she's with a female friend, so you bring a buddy with you to make it a two-on-two encounter. While your buddy (your wingman) chats up the friend, you get the undivided attention of the one you're interested in.

In scenarios like these you are known as the "primary," while your wingman provides "cover fire." Your wingman might be interested in the girl's friend, or he might just pretend to be interested in order to keep her occupied. (If the girlfriend is unattractive, we refer to it as "taking one for the team." If she's a 1 on the 10 scale, you're "jumping on a live grenade.")

But this is just the first step of a successful winging operation. The average guy thinks it's only about providing a distraction and figures that any available buddy of his can wing him at a moment's notice. But being a wingman isn't simply about providing a distraction. It's about making the primary shine.

As a Mack, you need to know proper wingman technique for two reasons: so that you can coach your friends to wing you in the most effective manner possible, and so that you can return the favor when they require it. As a Mack, you shouldn't hesitate to help out a brother in arms.

For starters, do not use a wingman if you are approaching a solitary female. You're much better off approaching her alone. Two men trying to engage her at the same time will make her uncomfortable. There's simply too much testosterone flying, and too much information for her to process.

Use a wingman when you want to approach a girl who is accompanied by one or more friends. *But never go into battle with a wingman who isn't properly trained.* By "trained," we mean someone who understands you and knows how to help you achieve your objectives. The skilled wingman will steer the conversation toward your good qualities, allowing you to talk about your strong points without sounding like you're bragging. Conversely, if you have vulnerable spots, the skilled wingman will make sure the conversation stays away from them.

Just as you shouldn't lie about yourself to a woman, your wingman should never lie on your behalf. As your friend, he should already know your positive qualities. He shouldn't need to make phony statements about how much money you've got or what you do for a living. These lies will only come back to bite you.

Let's say two Macks, Bob and Larry, are hanging out at a bar scoping women. Bob sees one who he's interested in (a beautiful blonde), but she's sitting at a table with a girlfriend (a mediocre brunette). So he tells Larry he wants to go for the blonde and asks him to wing him. Even though Larry isn't interested in the brunette, he's going to take one for the team. He knows Bob will do the same for him next time they're out macking together.

They approach the two women and strike up a conversation. Bob and Larry are paying equal attention to them at first; there's no sense that Bob is going to make a play for the blonde, or that Larry is going to isolate the brunette. It seems like a friendly group convo.

But throughout this convo, Larry is dropping gems—making subtle comments that make Bob shine. Because he's known Bob for years, he's knows his friend's good qualities:

- **He stays in good shape.**
- **He graduated from a good college.**
- **He has an interesting job.**
- **He just moved into a nice new apartment.**

Armed with this information, Larry can drop gems during their conversation with the girls:

> "I'm just glad Bob could come out tonight. Between his job and getting his new apartment set up, we haven't hung out in a while."

> "So you two are students at the university? Bob, you graduated from some really good school, didn't you?"

> (Referring to Bob): "I wasn't going to come out tonight, but I couldn't turn down hanging out with this guy. He always shows me a good time."

> "My job's going okay, but I'd rather be doing what Bob does for a living."

By making statements like these, Larry is shifting attention toward Bob and opening gateways for conversation that make him look good. Bob gets to talk a little bit about his new apartment, the college he went to, or his interesting job. A skilled wingman is like an All-Star point guard, feeding passes to his teammate that enable him to make baskets. But he does it subtly. It never sounds like Larry is making a "sales pitch" about what an awesome guy Bob is.

After a period of group conversation, Larry takes his winging mission to the next step. He shifts his body toward the brunette and asks her a direct question (i.e., "So what do you think of this place?"). In doing so, he creates a one-on-one conversation with her.

Bob reads this cue. It's "go time." He focuses his attention on the blonde and starts a separate conversation with her.

The foursome has "naturally" seemed to split into two pairs. A few minutes later, Larry takes the brunette to the dance floor, leaving Bob and the blonde to get to know each other better.

On the dance floor, Larry is winging like a pro. He's being extra charming and funny with the brunette. He mentions that he and Bob have been best friends for years and that he can count on Bob for anything. The brunette is excited and flattered, since usually when they go out, guys only focus on her beautiful blonde friend. Larry is making sure they have a great time—dirty dancing with her, making her feel like they're totally hitting it off. Larry still has no interest in hooking up with her, but he knows that as a wingman he must "win her over" if Bob is going to succeed tonight. At any time, the brunette could decide to leave and take her beautiful friend with her.

When they take a break from dancing, before Larry takes her to the bar to get a drink, he stops by the table where Bob and the blonde are chatting. "Your friend is really cool," Larry says to the blonde. "We're going to get a drink at the bar. You guys enjoy yourselves."

Then Larry takes the brunette over to the bar, where they continue to talk and laugh. He knows how important it is that they appear to be having a ball together. Why? Because Larry is playing upon the competitive nature of females. When the blonde sees how well they're "hitting it off," it's going to encourage her to step it up a notch with Bob. She won't want her friend to be the only one who has fun tonight.

The above is an example of skilled winging. It's not something you're likely to see often. You're much more likely to see an unskilled wingman saying the wrong things and damaging his buddy's chances, or even worse, two guys trying to mack the same girl—which makes her feel like a piece of meat that a couple of dogs are scrapping over.

One of the biggest obstacles men face in social situations is the "unattractive friend," the one who gets jealous when her girlfriend is being macked on. The unattractive friend will interrupt and say she needs to go to the bathroom, or she needs to get home, or that the club is lame and they should go somewhere else. Anything to disrupt the guy's game and keep her friend from being the only one to hook up.

But not in the situation we described above. By "winning over" the brunette, Larry removed that obstacle from Bob's mission. He knew how to occupy her for as long as Bob needed him to. When Bob eventually asked the blonde back to his place, she said she needed to check with her friend first (women will *always* check with their friend). But instead of it being an obstacle, it wasn't even an issue. The brunette was happy to stay at the bar with Larry; he told her he'd give her a ride home later, no problem. This freed up Bob and the blonde to leave together.

An unskilled wingman, on the other hand, can blast you right out of the sky. Never forget that when you step to one or more women with a wingman at your side, the things he says and does reflect on you. If he says anything stupid or offensive, or is annoying in any way, it's a strike against both of you.

If you haven't used a guy as your wingman before, don't assume that because he's your friend that he's going to help you out, or even knows how to. Men are also competitive by nature. Some will put you down in front of women to make themselves look better. They might dominate the conversation and push you into the background, or even start hitting on the girl you're interested in. A guy can be a close friend of yours and still be a terrible wingman. In the presence of hammers he might abandon the "mission" and want to be the center of attention instead.

Here's another saying to keep in mind: "The man who acts as his own lawyer has a fool for a client." When you're in court, you want a good lawyer at your side because he makes you appear more credible. He backs up your story and stresses that whatever you're saying is true. Good lawyers have a way of "winning over" the jury. The jurors start to think, "If this intelligent, respectable, sharp-looking guy believes with all his heart that the defendant is innocent, then he probably is."

Think of your wingman as your lawyer. While you're chatting with a woman, you're laying out your story: who you are and what you have to offer. It's the wingman's job to help her believe that you are the great guy you appear to be. At the same time, the wingman should be presenting himself as a cool, respectable guy. She should be thinking to herself about you, "If he has friends like this, that think so highly of him, then he must be something special."

Once you and your wingman make your approach on two women and the conversation begins, the wingman should follow your lead. If you drop hints about where you want the conversation to go, he should read these signals and assist you. The commandment "Three-quarters of macking is listening" definitely applies to winging. He should say nothing to make you feel awkward. You can *pretend* to feel a little bit embarrassed when he mentions your strong points—playing it "modest"—but you should be expecting every gem he drops.

In some situations, you and your buddy will approach two women without knowing which one you're going to go for; perhaps they're both attractive and the two of you want to feel it out, see if either woman shows a positive reaction to one of you. In this situation the two of you are essentially winging each other.

While the two of you are conversing with the women, watch their eyes and body language. The guy she makes more eye contact with, and possibly shifts her body toward, is the one she is interested in. If the girl you want is interested in your buddy, don't get competitive. Wing him. Have the group conversation, then isolate the other girl so that the group splits up into two pairs. You will either invite your girl to another part of the room (the bar, the dance floor, etc.), or your buddy will do so with his girl.

In situations in which you are winging, you'll find yourself trying to occupy a girl who doesn't want to be talked to. View it as a fun challenge. Propose a hypothetical and try to engage her. A truly skilled wingman can always find a way to entertain a girl so that his buddy can achieve his mission.

Sometimes your best efforts as a wingman won't be enough. You can't distract a girl who is determined to be obnoxious and blow you off. If she's giving you these vibes, don't stick around. The situation will only get more awkward. Abort your mission. Tell the girls it was nice meeting them, give your primary a nod, and excuse yourself. He'll have to handle this one solo. It won't be easy, but it can be done.

If you've been dating a girl, you're eventually going to introduce her to your friends. If they're solid wingmen, they're going to go out of their way to make her feel comfortable and part of the group. They should mention how you've told them good things about her. They should make sure she's never lacking for a drink. They should include her in the conversation, and make sure she's never left without someone to talk to if you need to leave the group for a few minutes. As a Mack, you'll do the same for a girl that one of your friends brings out.

14

Closing the Deal

> **Mack Fact: On average, human beings will have sex more than 3,000 times and spend two weeks kissing in their lifetime.**

It's Saturday night and Mike is at a nightclub. He's deep into a conversation with a hammer named Erica and everything is going beautifully. She was with a girlfriend when Mike first noticed her, but his wingman Bill was able to remove her from the equation. While Bill is on the dance floor distracting the friend, Mike has been chatting with Erica at a table in back.

They've been talking nonstop for an hour and seem to have a million things in common. Mike has been using conversation control to keep the discussion fun and stimulating. He has engaged her mind with original topics and entertained her with a few hypotheticals. He slipped in some of his strong points, while avoiding any topics that might burst the romantic bubble he's constructing. Erica wasn't in the mood to meet any new men when she showed up tonight—she explained that she's still getting over a bad breakup—but Mike has taken her mind off "that guy." Now, she's focused on him. Because of the conversational techniques he's been using, Erica feels that Mike is . . . well, *different*. In a good way. He's not like the other guys who approach her at these places. He has a broad range of interests and seems genuinely interested in what she has to say.

Mike checks his watch. It's 12:45; last call for alcohol is in fifteen minutes. He considers asking her to continue the conversation back at his place, but doesn't want to sound too forward. He figures there's no need to rush things—she seems totally into him, and seeing her again shouldn't be a problem. He takes out his cell phone and asks her for her phone number. She gives it to him. Mike figures he'll call her in a couple of days, invite her to dinner, and make some magic happen then. They say good night, she gives him a nice long kiss, and Mike figures he has a hot date to look forward to.

But it doesn't work out that way. Mike calls her the following evening and leaves a message on her machine. No reply. He calls her again the next day; this time she answers. She sounds surprised to hear from him, but not in a good way— more like she's trying to remember who he is. Mike had gathered his intel and knows she's free on Saturdays, so he suggests they have some sushi at a new restaurant he's heard great things about. But she says she just started a new job and will be really busy for the next couple of weeks. The conversation ends awkwardly and abruptly.

When Mike hangs up, he's pissed off and confused. How could she seem so into him at the club, and then blow him off two days later?

Here's the reality: when some girls give out their phone number, they expect you to call them and are hoping you'll ask them out. But then there are girls like Erica: one-night-only opportunities. She was ready and willing to go home with Mike that night, but he failed to read the signals. He thought he was playing it cool, but in reality he played himself.

The moral of the story is this: if the opportunity is there, you need to make your move *that night.*

Depending on the circumstances, getting her phone number might be your only option that night. She might have mentioned that she has to be at work early in the morning. She might need to give her friend a ride home and therefore can't leave with you. Maybe you met her at the mall, and clearly you're not going to take her home straight from the Gap store. Or maybe *you* have something to do in the morning that means you need to go home and get some sleep. But if the situation is right, know that *that night* is your best and perhaps only opportunity to make magic happen. Closing the deal is about knowing how to read signals and capitalize.

Why did Erica blow Mike off on the phone? Because she was in a completely different frame of mind forty-eight hours after their first encounter. She was no longer in the romantic bubble; she was back to dealing with the pressures of her job, her pain-in-the-ass roommate, and her stalker exboyfriend trying to get back with her. When Mike called, she didn't remember him as that charming guy she hit it off with. Her brain registered him as "the guy from the club." (Sounds sort of seedy, doesn't it?) She remembers they had a fun time chatting—but then again, her female instincts tell her, that could have been the alcohol.

When Mike called her, her mind started dwelling on negative possibilities. Does she really want to go on a date with some guy she met at a *nightclub*? He's trying to ask her out; is she going to have to give out her home address so that he can pick her up? What if he's a stalker, like her ex? It's a whole lot easier for her to make up an excuse and get rid of him. Besides, she can always meet another guy when she goes out tonight.

You need to be aware that no matter how heavy the sparks are flying, if the night ends with an exchange of phone numbers a future date is by no means assured. By using conversation control, she is far more likely to remember the great time she had with you and agree to a date. But it's not guaranteed. We can't begin to tell you how many guys we've heard complain about this: they meet a girl, hit it off, spend a bunch of money on drinks, and exchange phone numbers at the end of the night. But when they call, she acts completely different. She barely wants to speak with them, let alone make dinner plans.

This is why you need to lay groundwork, and if possible, close the deal that night.

Probing Questions

How far is she willing to go with you tonight? Is she spontaneous and free-spirited, or is she cautious? You can gain these answers by asking probing questions.

The first probing question you should ask is whether

she's in a relationship or not. Ask in a playful way, with a smile. Your inquiry should sound flattering and respectful, not intrusive. The key with this probing question is not to ask it too soon, as it will make you look overeager. But you also don't want to ask too late in the conversation, by which point you may have wasted precious time. The rule of thumb is to ask this question approximately seven minutes into the convo. We're not saying you need to check your stopwatch. Go with the flow, keeping this general time frame in mind.

Remember, there is absolutely no harm in asking this question. If you fail to ask it, the longer the conversation goes the more you'll be wondering about her status. Better to get this out of the way so that you can relax and settle into a comfortable groove, knowing what your options are.

Wack Tactic: "So do you have a boyfriend?"
Mack Tactic: "I'm really enjoying talking to you. I'm just wondering if you're spoken for."

(Note the phrase "spoken for." It sounds old-fashioned and extracourteous, something women appreciate. It's also an original bit of phrasing.)

Or, if you're in a party environment, try this gem: "Your man must be really secure to let a beautiful woman like you come here without him."

If she tells you that she has a boyfriend/husband, plan on making a graceful exit within the next few minutes. The key word here is "graceful." Never give the sense that you're leaving just because of her answer. Tell her, "It's still a pleasure meeting someone like you." Maintain your friendly, casual vibe, and it will eliminate any awkward feelings. If you appear comfortable with her reply, she'll become more comfortable with you. In fact, it may cause her to feel a sense of relief now that her status is out in the open. Think how awkward it must feel for a woman, when a guy is chatting with her at length and she knows at some point she'll have to burst his bubble and mention her man.

If she says she's spoken for, in no way is this a rejection. She may find you highly appealing, but she's faithful to her significant other and is being honest about it. You can't knock a woman for that.

You don't want to waste your time hanging around this unavailable woman, but you *do* want to make sure that you leave a positive impression. Spend a few more minutes chatting with her. By befriending her, making it clear that you have no expectations, you make her your ally. She might actually wind up winging you when you talk to another female tonight! She knows she won't be hooking up with anyone at this place, and women often get a kick out of winging a nice guy. It can even turn into a little game between the two of you; she helps you scope out another attractive girl to talk to. It *never* hurts to have an attractive female ally in any environment you're in, especially if you showed up without one.

If she hesitates and smiles before saying she's spoken for, or gives an awkward explanation (i.e., "I'm *sort of* seeing someone"), then consider her fair game. She has doubts about the guy she's currently with and is open to better offers. And if she says she's single, take it as a sign that she wants you to know she is fully available.

Another purpose of probing questions is to make her state something about herself that you can then hold her to.

This is a common hostage negotiation technique. The negotiator will say something to the hostage taker like, "Ed, it sounds to me like you're a man of your word. Is this true?" Ninety-nine percent of the time Ed will say yes. The negotiator then uses this as a recurring theme throughout the convo: Ed is a Man of his Word. By reminding him of this, the negotiator makes Ed more likely to behave in this manner.

If the negotiator gets Ed to say he agrees to something— i.e., that he won't hurt the hostages as long as the cops don't try to hurt him—the negotiator will remind Ed about this if he starts making threats: "I know you're a man of your word, Ed. And you gave me your word about not hurting the hostages."

When dealing with the females, use the same technique but focus on *spontaneity*. Give her a sly smile and say, "Tina, I get the impression that you're a spontaneous type of girl. Am I right?"

If she answers yes, that's great—you're dealing with a live wire who has the potential to be a lot of fun. If she hesitates and says, "I don't know. I guess sometimes," then follow up with another playful question: "What's the most spontaneous thing you've ever done?" Get her to admit this side of herself. *Get her in a spontaneous frame of mind.*

Now, as far as the two of you are concerned, she's no longer just Tina. She is Tina the Spontaneous. Later on, when you suggest that the two of you go somewhere together, she's more likely to forget her doubts and concerns and display her fun, spontaneous side—the side that you are encouraging.

The third probing question you can ask (always delivered with a smile): "So what time's your curfew?" It's a funny, out-of-left-field question that makes women laugh. It also usually triggers a defensive response. Women want to portray themselves as independent. She'll probably say something like, "What do you mean, 'curfew'? I haven't had a curfew since I was sixteen!"

Smile and say, "That's good to know," then move on to the next subject. You've planted another seed that you can refer to later.

Use these three probing questions to establish that she is (A) single, (B) spontaneous, and (C) prepared to make this a late night. She's basically admitted that she's ready to have a good time with the right guy. Stick with your M.A.C.K. Tactics, and that guy is going to be you.

Body Contact

You already know the importance of smiling and maintaining eye contact during the conversation. Body contact is how you accelerate the encounter and move toward closing the deal.

The first step is closing the physical gap between you. If you're chatting with her at a bar, move closer to her and angle your body so that you're "shielding" her from the other men in the area. If you're sitting with her in a booth, scoot in closer so that your leg is touching hers. If it's a loud environment, speak close to her ear and have her speak into yours.

Wait at least ten minutes into a good, animated conversation to see if she makes body contact with you. Oftentimes, a woman will make body contact subconsciously if she is interested in you. Remember that even the most subtle, innocent-seeming touch sends a signal.

For instance, while she's laughing, she may reach over

and squeeze your arm. Or, she might touch your hand while she's making a point about something. Read these signals. A woman who is uninterested will avoid all body contact, while an interested woman will be comfortable making contact. Watch for cues; she'll give them to you.

Also note her body language. As you converse, is she leaning toward you, like she's interested in every word you say? Or is she keeping her distance? If she's sitting down, check her legs; they contain the most powerful muscles in the body. The way her legs are crossed is a gauge of her comfort level. Are they in a protective, businesslike position, literally blocking her private parts? Are her arms folded across her chest, meaning she's blocking her breasts and her heart?

If her body language is closed and defensive, don't worry. Some women are naturally on guard. It means you need to keep building the bridge of trust, knock down those barriers, and get her to loosen up.

If she's acting tense, make a playful comment about it. She might not even realize she's giving off these vibes. When you mention it, she'll switch to a more relaxed posture if she is interested in you. If she stays in a defensive posture, you know you're facing an uphill battle. You'll want to consider cutting your losses, politely excusing yourself, and having a good time with someone else.

If ten minutes pass and she hasn't made any physical contact with you whatsoever—but you feel the encounter has potential—it's time for you to take the lead and make the initial contact. The simplest way to do this is to reach over and lightly touch her forearm. Do it in mid-sentence, as if to emphasize what you're saying. Don't let the touch linger too long; simply establish that first contact. It opens an important subliminal door.

When she says something funny, you can reach over and touch her arm while the two of you are laughing. Or, if you're making a point about something, place your hand on top of hers. Make it seem like you did it on reflex. Don't keep it there long; *just make that contact.*

Most men don't take the time to *build* physical connections. Instead of dancing with women, they try to grind on them like dogs in heat. Instead of giving a soft good-night kiss, they want to stick their tongue in her mouth. By establishing gentle body contact, you're giving her the chance to grow accustomed to your touch and feel comfortable with it. More intimate touching can follow. Take it in steps.

Once you're deep in conversation, and you can sense the chemistry building, another way to establish body contact is to say, "Let me see your hands." If she asks why, tell her, "I'm a hand person, I'm really into hands."

Most women take care with their hands and want to be sure they look and feel nice. When she offers her hands to you, gently take them in your hands, give them a caress, and turn them over to check out the flip side. Pay her a compliment: "I like your hands. It looks like you take good care of them."

While you might need to wait until the end of the evening to go for a kiss, you can ensure that kiss by making sure she has become physically comfortable with you. This is accomplished by making body contact through the course of the evening. Touching hands leads to holding hands. Touching her arm leads to putting your arm around her, or gently playing with her hair. Sitting close to her, so that your legs are touching, leads to you placing a hand on her thigh. Be slow but methodical, and note how she responds to every step. It should feel like a natural progression.

Talking Dirty

> **Mack Fact: Humans and dolphins are the only species that have sex for pleasure.**

Some guys think it's okay to talk about sex with girls they've just met. They steer the conversation toward sex, or make sexual comments in an attempt to be funny and "spice up" the convo. Other guys think that talking about sex implies they have a lot of experience in the bedroom, and that women will find this alluring.

Women are generally *not* interested or impressed by this type of talk. More likely, they'll think it's crude and juvenile. (Besides, guys who hook up on a regular basis don't need to boast about it.)

But you can get her mind on erotic thoughts. The key is to do it in a clever, "invisible" way. As the conversation progresses, test the waters to see how receptive she is to talking about sexual topics. Scan the room. Do you see any couples kissing or dirty dancing? If so, direct her attention to the couple and ask her with a smile, "What do you think about them doing that in a public place?"

If she has no problem with it—or even better, is intrigued by it—then the door is open for you to touch on other sexual topics. Roll with it. Here are a couple of ways to spark the convo:

- Ask her how she defines the word "sexy." After she answers, tell her that in your opinion, sexiness isn't about how someone looks on the surface—it's about confidence and attitude. Women like this answer. Few women are totally confident in their appearance, but all women like to believe they have confidence and a good attitude.
- Ask her what she thinks is the sexiest part of her body. After she answers, tell her that you couldn't help noticing that part of her—but there is *another* body part that you really find appealing. This could be her eyes, teeth, hair, neck . . . there is no standard answer. This should sound genuine, not canned. This type of unexpected compliment should flatter her. It also shows that you're not judging her by the obvious standards (breasts, body, etc.) that most men do.

The Kiss

Anyone who's a great kisser,
I'm always interested in.
—Cher

The first kiss, obviously, is huge. For the average guy, getting to this kiss is like driving in the dark without directions. They're hoping that if they drive around long enough, they'll eventually wind up at their destination—trying not to crash in the meantime.

Kissing can be easy if you're in a party atmosphere

where drinks are being consumed. It's an environment that encourages spontaneous behavior and impulsive makeout sessions. But it's much different when you're on a date with a girl who you haven't kissed yet. If nothing else, you might want to get the kiss out of the way so that the two of you can be at ease with each other. That first kiss changes the whole dynamic, relieving the pressure and opening up a world of possibilities.

You want to get there as soon as possible; playing too long in pre-kiss purgatory is a dangerous game. But at the same time it should never seem like you're rushing it. If she rejects your attempt to kiss her, it's an awkward moment for both of you that kills the mood. It might ruin your chances of ever getting one.

Getting this kiss is all about laying down the right groundwork. You build a bridge toward it by gradually escalating your amount of contact with her. It begins with eye contact and smiles and graduates to body contact: your hand touching hers, putting your hand on the small of her back while ushering her through a door, leaning in and speaking softly into her ear when you want to tell her a private joke.

At the same time, it's important to plant the seed that you are a clean person and have good oral hygiene. This may sound funny, but it's no laughing matter to women. Until you've kissed, your mouth and breath are two big question marks in her mind. Eliminate any doubts by inserting hints into the conversation.

Pop a breath mint, offer her one, and casually mention how you always try to keep your breath fresh. You can even relate a quick story about an attractive girl you went on a date with, but her breath turned you off. Don't linger on the subject, just plant the seed.

Keep laying groundwork. During dinner, do a quick check of your silverware and glass. Make sure they're clean. Say, "I like this place, it's always very clean." Again, you're reinforcing in her subconscious that you care about cleanliness. Your mouth isn't something to be unsure about.

For the same reasons, Christopher always keeps some hand sanitizer in his car. Not only does it make him feel fresh and help his Mack mind-set, but it also makes an impression on women when they ride in his car.

Read her signals, the way she responds to your eye and body contact. Keep building that bridge. If the two of you have been locking eyes and smiling during your conversations, and she's comfortable with the subtle body contact you are establishing, then you're successfully building the bridge toward the kiss. The kiss shouldn't feel like a "leap." It should be the natural next step.

Neutral Corners

With a girl you've met that evening—let's say at a nightclub or party—you're better off taking her somewhere "neutral" before trying to bring her back to your place. If possible, suggest going for some coffee, getting a bite to eat, or taking a walk outside. This additional step creates the sense that the two of you are on a date, even if you just met an hour before. It also makes her feel more secure. You're not rushing things; you're letting the evening unfold at its own pace.

Just remember that women know the deal just as well as

you do. Don't feel embarrassed about your intentions. You're both adults. She knows that you're a heterosexual guy and your end goal lies in the bedroom. If you've laid the necessary groundwork, making her feel attractive, comfortable, and spontaneous, then she'll be looking forward to it, too. Perhaps not on the first night, but that door will eventually open.

She should feel that she has nothing to worry about with you. For this reason, *you should always take her back to your place instead of trying to go to hers.* For a lot of women, bringing a guy home is a big deal. It means you know where she lives, and she might not be comfortable with that until she knows you better. She's much more likely to accept an invitation to go to your place than she is to invite you to hers.

If you don't live in a place you can bring girls home to, then as a Mack you need to fix this ASAP. In order to be an effective Mack, you *must* have a home base where you can host women. In the "Mi Casa, Mack Casa" chapter, we'll break this down.

Go with the Flow

Even if she's up for a one-night stand, and the encounter appears to be heading in that direction, most women don't want to *feel* like it's going to be a one-night stand. While men brag to their buddies about these casual conquests, women have been raised to believe that it's wrong and slutty.

While they may do it, they don't always feel good about it afterward.

One way to cushion this is to establish a "next meeting" during the initial conversation: the idea that regardless of how tonight winds up, the two of you are going to meet again in the near future. She may be thinking the same thing you are—one night, no strings attached—but the idea of a "next meeting" may help put her mind at ease.

The concept is simple. During your chat, mention a movie that's in theaters right now and how you want to see it. Say "maybe we'll go see it together." Or, mention a restaurant you like and say "we should go sometime." Then move on to another subject. You're not setting up an actual date; you're planting the seed that you would be open to seeing her after tonight.

Some women might ask you point-blank, "Is this just going to be a one-night thing?" You have to have an answer ready for this. This is how Christopher replies: "A couple of years ago, my answer might have been yes. But that's not what I'm into now. I think we might have something going on here and I'd like to go with it, see what happens."

With this answer, again, you're not making any promises. You're just going with the flow and encouraging her to do the same. It's too early to know if this is going to turn into an ongoing relationship.

Blame It on the Rain:
The Milli Vanilli Principle

So in a laid-back, no-strings-attached kind of way, you make the offer that will get both of you back to your place. If it's getting late and you are at a bar/nightclub/party: "I'm getting a little tired of this scene. Let's do something else." Your inflection is important. Never sound like you're bored or complaining. Say it playfully. You're a train that is ready to roll on to the next adventure, and you want her to come along.

This will prompt her to ask, "What do you want to do?" or "Where do you want to go?"

"We can go somewhere else like this," you tell her, "but the loud music is kind of getting to me." (Depending on the environment, instead of music you can substitute the words *smoke* or *crowd*.)

With this answer, you don't seem like you're in a hurry to move things back to your place. You're "open" to any number of options. Subliminally, however, the message you are sending is that you don't want to go to another bar/nightclub/party, because those environments are too loud, smoky, or crowded. You want to go somewhere quieter. Your home is the obvious solution.

If she wants to spend more time with you, it's time for you to take the lead and suggest this. Don't feel awkward about this next move. You know the deal. *She* knows the deal. The key is to phrase the invitation in a way that makes her feel comfortable. She doesn't want to feel like sex is assumed.

Tell her there's something you'd love to show her. It's something back at your place: a painting, a photograph, a book, etc. If you've enjoyed some wine with her at dinner, you can invite her to try a good bottle you've got at home.

Ideally, it's an area that the two of you have a common interest in. If you discussed your mutual love of a certain type of music, it could be a CD you want to play for her. If she dug the fact that you play guitar, you might offer to play her a song you just learned. If she was interested in that trip you took to Europe, tell her you want to show her some pictures. Be enthusiastic and convey the feeling that this is something you want to *share* with her. It doesn't need to be something incredibly impressive. Again, she knows the deal. If she wants to come home with you, you simply need to give a reason.

You don't want to say, "Let's go back to my place." This point-blank suggestion might work if she's really into you, but even then women prefer to be led gently down this path. And even if she's anticipating the invite, she may have concerns in the back of her mind. She doesn't want to seem "easy." In fact, if she really likes you, she may be apprehensive about going home with you because she wants to date you in the future. She doesn't want you to view her as a one-night stand.

In hostage negotiations, the negotiator never asks the hostage taker, "Are you ready to surrender?" This is because the word "surrender" carries negative connotations. It's basically asking him to give up and come out with his tail between his legs.

Instead, the negotiator cushions the suggestion: "Listen, John, are you ready to come out? We've worked together as a team tonight. I want you to do the right thing."

As a Mack, you cushion the suggestion by offering to share something that has meaning to you. Like the negotiator, work her name into your invitation. If she agrees, you can smile and throw in a quick joke to set the tone for the rest of the night: fun and casual. Try using one of these:

"Just promise you won't take advantage of me."
"Just promise you won't make any jokes about my place. I haven't cleaned it in a few days." (This also makes it seem like you had no intention of bringing a girl back to your place tonight. You're just going with the flow.)

If the night results in sex, she should feel like it was a "happy accident," that you didn't have any agenda . . . things just *happened.* After being with a Mack, the woman should feel that sex was the natural conclusion. There's no need for anyone to feel guilty about anything. There was nothing seedy about it. A good time was had by all.

Christopher likes to use the expression "blame it on the rain." For those of you who still dig the music of 1980s (or watch too much VH-1), you'll know it's a reference to the Grammy Award–winning tune by Milli Vanilli. While the infamous lip-synching duo aren't remembered for their lyrical genius, that particular song does contain some clever romantic insights. The verses are about various romantic occurrences. The chorus basically says that there's no need for deep thought or explanation; when the chemistry is right, just go for it. There's really no way to explain it. You might as well "blame it on the rain."

That's how she should feel the next morning. There

wasn't any pressure coming from your end. The two of you hit it off and nature took its course.

If you lay the right groundwork and guide the encounter along, women will be willing to take the ride with you. It's then up to you whether you want to pursue the relationship further.

15

Mi Casa, Mack Casa

As a Mack, your home is your castle, your sanctuary, the headquarters from which you launch your missions. It's also where you're going to close the deal with most women, since she's much more likely to come back to your place than to invite you to hers. This means your living quarters are an essential part of your overall Mack package.

Show us a man whose home is a pigsty, and we'll show you a man who has given up with women. Obviously, he doesn't expect to bring any home, so why bother keeping it clean? The Mack, meanwhile, maintains a clean, comfortable abode at all times. It's about more than being ready to host female company; it's also about maintaining a positive, confident mind-set. If you surround yourself with crap, you're going to feel like crap. And if you leave the house knowing you can't bring home female company, you never will.

Whenever you manage to get a girl back to your place, you're winning the ball game. At this point it isn't necessary for you to dazzle her. Your home simply needs to meet certain standards. If it doesn't, don't be surprised if she makes up an excuse to cut out early. She sees your home as a reflection of you: is it comfortable and inviting, or is it dirty and in disarray?

Just as you are taking steps to improve your attitude, your conversational skills, and your appearance, you must make an assessment of your home and begin making adjustments and improvements. We're not talking about a top-to-bottom overhaul, like you've been invaded by the *Queer Eye for the Straight Guy* gang. Instead, we're going to lay out some simple guidelines. After all, it's important that your home reflects who you are and what you're about.

Discard any decorations you're still clinging to from your youthful party days. Street signs, neon beer signs, and posters involving hot chicks or alcoholic beverages are unacceptable. In fact, you shouldn't hang any posters at all unless they are framed. (The same goes for photographs.) Forget about using plastic crates as furniture, or to hold your overflowing piles of CDs or DVDs. Buy a shelving unit, or store them in a trunk and keep them out of sight.

As far as furniture and decorations, anything old or ratty-looking has to go. That means the shower curtain with the stains on it, the dirty doormat, the couch with holes in it, etc. It's better to take a minimalist approach—a few nice pieces of furniture—than to have multiple chairs, couches, tables, etc. that look like you bought them at a yard sale.

Obviously, your income level, as well as your age, will be a determining factor in how you rearrange your place. If you're twenty-three years old, women will expect you to live differently than if you are forty-five.

Here's a basic breakdown of what women will typically expect of your home, based on your age:

Under 25: Fortunately, you can get away with a lot. Women expect that you're still in a post-college phase, making your transition into the adult world. Living with multiple roommates is acceptable, as long as the place is reasonably clean and your area is tidy. It's okay to still be living with your parents, but you'd better start making plans to move out. You can't be a Mack when your mom is baking brownies in the next room.

26–30: You shouldn't be living at home with your parents, and shouldn't have more than one roommate. You must have your own bathroom and phone line. Living with a bunch of guys, even if it's in a big house with plenty of space, is a red flag for women—it's a sign of emotional immaturity and that drinking beer with the boys is still your priority.

Over 30: You're past the roommate thing. You've got a bachelor pad with decent furniture and a complete kitchen. (Even if you don't cook, you must have nice dishes and utensils, as well as all the basic appliances so that you can invite a woman over for a meal.)

Decorating Sense

How you decorate your home is a matter of personal taste. Like with fashion, we don't believe it's appropriate for us to make specific suggestions unless we know *you* as an individual—what works with your personality, and what brings out your best. But we can certainly advise you on things to avoid. The following are the top-five date killers:

1. **Filth and funky odors**
2. **Inappropriate items**
3. **Clutter**
4. **Other people in the house**
5. **An overly romantic theme**

Each one of these on their own can kill a date. Some guys have a combination of all of them, which is enough to send a woman fleeing in horror. Let's break each one down and work toward solutions.

Filth and Funky Odors

If you've lived in an unclean environment for a long time, you're no longer aware of how unpleasant it may smell. (It's the same principle as bad breath; you can't smell your own, but the ladies pick it up from five feet away.) Empty your wastepaper baskets and trash cans and keep dirty dishes in the dishwasher. Bacteria is what creates the stink. When a girl (or anyone for that matter) enters your home, it should instantly strike her as a fresh-smelling location.

Experiment with different air fresheners. Advanced Macks may even use different types of smells depending on the time of day, or type of date. Try scented candles, oils, and incense, but be careful not to overdo it. Open the windows a minimum of twice a week to air the place out; if you don't, you're piling smells on top of stale air.

Next, we can't overstate the importance of a clean bathroom. Make that a *spotless* bathroom. She *will* ask to use it so she can freshen up, so it had better be ready. That means your toiletries are neatly arranged and your toilet and bathtub are both scrubbed clean. Keep some liquid hand soap next to your bathroom sink; show her that you care about cleanliness. For an added touch, place a scented candle and a book of matches on top of the toilet.

Inappropriate Items

Make sure any overtly sexual books, magazines, DVDs, or videotapes are well stashed. (Yes, this means your porn collection.) Don't forget to check your VCR or DVD player for something you might have left behind. Also make sure that all bills, mail, and financial statements are tucked away from prying eyes. If they're out in the open, she'll probably steal a look.

Give your bathroom a sweep and make sure any and all prescription medications are concealed. Anything that implies you are in less-than-perfect health works against you. Finally, hide any photos of ex-girlfriends (or current girlfriends, for that matter). You don't want to have to explain.

Clutter

If she has to navigate a minefield of CDs, books, and stray clothes to get to your couch, it's a serious problem. Stick all of that stuff in a closet, and organize it when you have time.

Other People

The whole idea is for you to be alone with her and create a comfortable vibe. Roommates kill this vibe and make her feel like an intruder instead of a welcome guest. Even if your roommate stays in his room and out of your way, she's going to be uncomfortable knowing that someone else is present. You're better off waiting for an evening when your house or apartment is going to be empty. If your roommates are impeding your success as a Mack, take action and figure out another living arrangement.

Overly Romantic Theme

Don't try *too* hard. Bringing a girl home to incense, burning candles, and a Barry White slow jam on the stereo is like saying, "Let's get it on . . . *right now*." If you haven't slept with her yet, she'll assume you're a "player" who uses this routine on every girl who comes over. No woman wants to feel like your next conquest. A clean, comfortable environment, combined with your Mack techniques and charming personality, is your recipe for romance.

But let's not forget several other important factors . . .

Lighting

This is essential for setting the mood. Don't rely on the bright overhead lights that came installed in your house or apartment. You can create a more intimate, relaxed environment by buying a couple of lamps with warm-colored lampshades and using lower-wattage lightbulbs. This is especially important in your bedroom, where you want to have a lighting option between bright overhead illumination and total darkness.

Wine

A Mack always has at least one bottle of wine on hand for female company. You don't need to be a connoisseur, and you don't need to shell out big bucks. The vast majority of women (and men) can't tell the difference between a bottle that costs $12.99 and one that costs $200.

Just keep it reasonably classy. Don't buy cheap hooch, and invest a few bucks in some decent wine glasses. If you're going to serve wine in a plastic cup, you might as well be serving malt liquor. Make sure your glasses are completely clean. She'll notice smudges and streaks—and she'll certainly notice another female's lipstick.

Offering her a glass of wine sets a nice tone: two sophisticated adults relaxing and enjoying each other's company. Serving beer is lowbrow, and offering a mixed drink with liquor is too much of a "party drink." You should, however, keep a selection of different liquors and mixers on hand, in case she prefers them to wine.

Have at least one bottle of red and one bottle of white wine on hand at all times. If the date is at her place, bringing a bottle with you is a classy move. Just remember that white wine is generally served chilled (from the refrigerator), while red wine is served at room temperature.

For the white wine, go with either Pinot Grigio, which has a crisp, refreshing taste, or Chardonnay, which is lighter and fruitier. For red wine, you can't go wrong with Merlot or Cabernet. All of these wines have inexpensive versions (under $20) that you can pick up at your local supermarket or liquor store.

If you're having wine with a meal, the "rules" used to say that red wine goes with red meat, and white wine goes with fish and white meats, such as chicken. The idea is that white wine will compliment, rather than overwhelm, a lighter dish. Red wine, which is heartier and more robust, goes better with stronger-tasting red meats.

Today, many chefs say that you should simply choose the type of wine you like best. Know those basic rules in case she asks for your suggestion. Otherwise, let her choose the type she prefers. You should do the same.

Artwork

Having some artwork on the walls can give your home a sophisticated touch and add unique flourishes. It can also make for interesting conversation. If your budget is limited, look to purchase cool paintings, sculptures, or framed photographs from local or unknown artists. Point these pieces out to her, and explain how they were done by a local artist who you think is talented and want to support. You can seem like a patron of the arts without having to spend much money.

Setting a Mack Mood

Once she has entered your apartment, give her a few minutes to adjust to the environment. Find something to do that gives her some space and allows her to take in her surroundings. Going into the kitchen to get some beverages is a good idea. Take your time. Let her get comfortable.

Your next move should be to sit down with her on the couch. Once you've settled in, this may seem like the right time to turn on the TV or put on a DVD.

Macks handle it differently. Just as some parents use the television to occupy their kids, too many guys use television to occupy their dates. As we explain in the upcoming "First Dates" chapter, taking her to a movie is never a smart option at that early stage. It's when you need to be strengthening your bridge with her, using M.A.C.K. Tactics. Sitting in the dark next to her, with both of you focusing on a screen for two hours, does little to advance your progress. For the same reason, settling in with her to watch a movie at your place is not the best way to proceed.

Putting on the right music can enhance the mood. But when it comes to choosing tunes, you must proceed with caution. Music inspires and moves most of us more than any other medium. In some cases, a song can trigger powerful memories and emotions. Before you reach for a CD, consider the full spectrum of possibilities. Maybe a sexy slow jam will get her juices flowing, but it might have an opposite effect. What if it's a song that she and her ex used to make love to? What if it's a song that reminds her of a painful breakup? Maybe she's getting comfortable with you, but she's not ready to get hot and heavy; in this case, putting on "seduction music" is going to make her feel uncomfortable, as if you expect sex to be the next step.

The Mack plays it smart and eliminates these risks. Instrumental mood music is your best bet: jazz, trance, laid-back electronica, or deep house. If you're not familiar with these types of music, make a trip to the record store. Music should provide a calming background for your conversation. It should never be a focal point or a distraction.

Instead of focusing on movies or music she knows the words to, you're going to focus on each other with interesting conversation. Kick off your shoes and ask her to do the same. Get comfortable on the couch. Now use a hostage negotiator technique called "refreshing" to keep things flowing: remember a topic that she brought up earlier and prompt her to keep talking about it. Guide the conversation in a direction that is going to make her smile rather than dwell on the negative. For example, "You mentioned during dinner that you're not all that happy where you're working. Tell me what your dream job would be."

Magazines are another way to keep the conversation flowing. Keep a few good titles on your coffee table, such as *GQ, Vanity Fair, Esquire, Men's Health,* and *Entertainment Weekly*. Nothing too sexual such as *Maxim* or *Playboy*. Having these magazines on your coffee table gives the impression that you enjoy reading and keeping up on things. Women love to browse through magazines; chances are she'll pick one up and start checking it out. Or, take the lead: flip to a page and ask her opinion about a certain story or celebrity. Her responses will provide more intel on her, about her likes and dislikes and her opinions on matters. Just make sure to skip over all subjects and advertisements that can damage the mood (i.e., condom ads, stories on violent subject matter, etc.). Keep it light and fun. Set the mood with the right lighting and some mellow music, keep the convo flowing, work the body contact, and good times should follow.

16

First Dates

All of the Mack techniques we're teaching you are ways of opening doors to first dates. Once she has agreed to "jump on your train," the most obvious question is where you should take her.

There are endless date possibilities when you follow Mack Commandment 6, "Be original." Instead of trying to list them all, we're going to start with three "don'ts."

Don't take her to:

1. The movies. This is where a lot of guys go for a "safe" first date. It's inexpensive (even with the overpriced sodas and popcorn) and doesn't require any planning other than checking the movie times. But think about the environment: you're sitting next to her for two hours in the dark and not talking. And there's nothing particularly memorable about a trip to the local multiplex.

2. Nightclubs. This can be a hazardous environment for a first date. Nightclubs are for meeting friends or for macking on someone new. If you visit one with your date, you're bound to see other girls you want to mack on. You'll be unfocused and your date will pick up on these vibes. Then there are the expensive drinks, lines for the bathroom, and often a lack of comfortable places to sit. The loud music makes it bad for conversation. Guys are all over the place, checking out your girl and waiting to move in if you leave her for five minutes. For these reasons and others, you'll want to steer clear of nightclubs on a first date.

3. Any event involving friends or family. At these get-togethers, there are politics going on that you have to deal with, and it's awkward (especially for her) when you have to constantly introduce her to people and have her try to remember names. You may find yourself having to apologize for the behavior of others, especially if the booze is flowing.

From her perspective, your family and friends are a reflection of you. You can't control their behavior, or how they will act toward your date. For these reasons, you shouldn't introduce her to these people until you've solidified your relationship with her. Don't let your obnoxious cousin or liquored-up buddy ruin *your* chances.

The bottom line is that on a first date, you must leave nothing to chance. It's possible that you could take her to one of these places and end up having a great time. But they do contain risks, and on a first date you want to do everything possible to ensure that it goes off without a hitch. You want to be in control of the environment so that you're focusing on each other instead of outside distractions. These three environments are ones in which you surrender control. There are many others. Be creative with the place you choose to take her, but always consider the "other variables" you may need to contend with.

Pickups

You'll always want to pick her up for the date rather than meeting her somewhere. This places you in the driver's seat in more ways than one.

Have the radio set to a popular station, but keep it at a low volume. Then ask her if there's something specific that she'd like to listen to: "I don't usually listen to the radio, so if you want to hear a station just let me know." The radio is a safer bet than putting on one of your CDs. She might not like the style of music you've chosen, but will probably be too polite to say anything. Let her put on her favorite radio station and enjoy the music she likes. It will brighten her mood.

If you drive a less-than-impressive car, just be sure it's clean—and know that a little air freshener can go a long way. If your car is an eyesore, or there's any chance that it will break down, take a taxi and explain to her that your car is in the shop—and know that as a Mack, you'll need to start looking into a better set of wheels ASAP. You certainly don't need to drive a tricked-out Escalade or a Benz, but you do need to have a decent, reliable vehicle. If you *do* happen to drive a nice car, downplay any compliments. Tell her, "I'm just glad it's reliable and gets me around."

Dinner Dates

Whether you're meeting for cocktails, coffee, or dinner, the place absolutely must be clean. Faced with a choice between great food or a clean environment, go for the clean environment. This is especially true when it comes to restaurants.

Before the date, you need to have your game plan worked out. If you're taking her to dinner, be familiar with the restaurant. If you haven't eaten there before, visit the restaurant prior to your date to scope it out. Know exactly where it is and the type of food it serves. If you don't have time to visit, call the restaurant, talk to a staff member, and ask some questions about their menu, their prices, and anything special they offer. You can also try looking it up on the Internet and learning some facts about the place and its owners. During the date, these are all good conversational topics. The more enthusiastic and knowledgeable you are about the restaurant, the more special the occasion will feel to her.

You should be familiar with a variety of restaurants, since women have different tastes. But have at least two staples. Sushi and Italian are good ones. If the staff knows you, and you know the menu, you'll look and feel in control of the environment. It's better to "master" two restaurants than to be somewhat familiar with joints all over town. If the restaurant has an attractive waitress or two, even better. If they remember you and greet you personally, your date will be impressed. Then again, a pretty waitress can be a macking option for the future. When you show up with an attractive date, you become more intriguing to that waitress. You might want to show up next time alone, or with a male friend, for the purposes of getting *her* phone number.

Before you go on this dinner date, walk through it in your mind. Know where you'd like to sit; there might be a nice outdoor area, or some comfortable booths. Also be aware of the parking options. If there is a valet, always use that option. It's a few bucks well spent.

Since originality is important, try to avoid chain restaurants. If you're on a tight budget, find a place to eat that is inexpensive but has interesting aspects that you can mention. This could be a special menu item, a certain dessert, or a quirky bit of history. Maybe back in the 1950s it was a Mafia hangout, or a famous movie filmed a scene there. You should be able to mention reasons why you picked this place. If you've eaten there in the past, mention that it's one of your "special places"—implying that you would only bring a special person there.

You might consider meeting her for drinks or a light meal at a casual restaurant, especially if you feel you don't know her that well yet. Even if money is not an object, taking her out to a fancy meal can backfire in several ways. Instead of impressing her, treating her to an expensive dinner (upward of $100) might actually make her feel uncomfortable: *I barely know this guy, and he's spending all this money. What is he going to expect at the end of the night?*

It also increases your own expectations. After shelling out big bucks on lobster and a good bottle of wine, you're going to feel cheated if you don't at least get a good-night kiss. You're also going to feel disappointed if ten minutes into the meal, you realize this isn't a woman you'd care to see again. Why put this added pressure on her, and on yourself?

For these reasons, it's usually better to keep this first meal relatively casual and low-cost. It shows that you aren't eager to make anything happen. The vibe you're sending is that you're interested in getting to know her; if a mutual attraction develops, you can always treat her to a nice meal next time. Spending excessive money can make you look like you're auditioning for the role of her boyfriend, trying to woo her by laying out cash.

As a rule of thumb, don't spend more than $60 on a first dinner unless you regularly spend that (or more) on meals. This first date sets the bar for how she expects your future dates to go, and she might not appreciate that bar being lowered. Once she associates you with gourmet cuisine, a burger joint is going to feel like a letdown.

Keep this first date simple and reasonable. If things go well, you can always take her to a more upscale restaurant in the future. It will then feel like a special occasion, instead of something she expects.

Etiquette Tips

Pull out the woman's chair and help her get seated. (In a more upscale restaurant, the host/hostess may take care of this.)

Shortly after sitting down, excuse yourself and say you'd like to wash your hands before you eat. This shows that you're concerned with cleanliness. Use some soap so that when you make hand contact with her, your skin feels soft and fresh.

Learn your server's name and use it when addressing him or her. It shows that you interact with people well and that you're polite.

Be open to suggestions. Your server may mention the evening's dinner specials. Listen, discuss them briefly with your date, and if something sounds good, go for it. This implies that you're spontaneous and not rigid in your choices.

You should order for yourself and for your date. Ask her what she wants as you're looking over your menus. It's then your job to tell the server what both of you will be having.

Pace your conversation during the meal. It's annoying when you're trying to eat and someone keeps asking you questions, so don't do it to her. During your meal, bear in mind Mack Commandment 8: "Three-quarters of macking is listening." Get into a rhythm with her; when she takes a bite, you take a bite. And pace yourself so that you don't finish eating long before she does.

Advance Mack Maneuver: Taste Tests

We've already covered the importance of establishing body contact as things progress. If you're having a great conversation over dinner and the two of you are obviously connecting, this can be done while sitting across from her at the table. Lean forward to tell her something, as if you don't want the people sitting around you to hear. Touch her forearm or hand when you say it.

Another way to establish contact during dinner is by tasting each other's food. Tell her how delicious yours is and offer her a bite—but do it right.

Don't cut off a piece and reach your fork across your table toward her mouth; that's an awkward gesture that puts her on the spot. Instead, cut off the piece of food, cup your hand underneath the fork, and offer it to her. It's an invitation she's not likely to turn down. Having shared the same fork (or spoon), you've established a subliminal physical bond. She'll probably then offer you a taste of hers. Your mouths, in a sense, have touched. This technique may sound funny, but these subtle connections can make a difference.

Or, you can test the waters first. Look at her meal and remark how good it looks. If she offers to give you a bite, that's a sign that she is comfortable with you. Give her a bite of yours in return.

Just Desserts

By all means, order dessert. This can be the most important phase of the meal. It's also the most appealing part. Everything about dessert is sexy, from the smell, to the rich taste, to the way it looks. Chocolate has actually been known to affect women's hormonal levels.

Practically all women love dessert, though some may try to decline because they're self-conscious about pigging out in front of you. Encourage her to go for it. If she still would rather not, order for yourself and request two forks. Order something rich and decadent. She'll be glad you did; few women can resist at least taking a bite.

If the menu has a description of the dessert you want, read it out loud: words like "chocolate," "strawberries," "ice cream," and "whipped cream" all have sexual connotations. Don't overdo it and let the words ooze out of your mouth. The subliminal messages are already strong.

Other Date Ideas

Dates don't need to begin after sundown. Most guys figure a date shouldn't start before 7 P.M., but if she expects to be home by midnight then you're limiting your time with her.

Daytime activities can extend the time frame. You can enjoy some activities together *and* have a meal.

Plan daytime dates around her interests. If she's into sports, consider taking her to a local high-school athletic event; the atmosphere will be filled with youthful energy and enthusiasm and may bring back fond memories of your own high-school days and romances.

Flea markets and swap meets can also be cool for an afternoon get-together. We all know how women love shopping, and these are a fun, low-cost way to browse for hours. It will also provide you with further intel; with dozens of different booths and endless wares for sale, you're going to find out her likes and dislikes, such as certain fragrances or types of artwork, furnishings, and jewelry. Walk with her through a swap meet, and you'll gain more knowledge about her than you would in five hours on the phone.

If you're an active person, a first date that allows you to

walk around with her can be a good idea. It's an even better idea if you tend to have a lot of nervous energy in these situations. Dinner requires you to park yourself in a chair and sit still for an hour. Walking will release this energy.

Browse your local newspapers, especially alternative ones that cover music and the arts. Keep your ears open for fairs or expos. Check out thrift and antique stores, art galleries, and cozy venues for live music. Consider taking her to stores and places that are interesting and off the beaten path, while avoiding malls, movie theaters, generic restaurants, and all the "usual" date locations.

Cancellations

On this first date, you want to make the best possible impression. You should be in an enthusiastic mood and ready to focus your full attention on her.

Sometimes, however, this just isn't possible. You might be having a terrible day, or dealing with a problem that is occupying your thoughts. Maybe something came up at work and you won't have enough time to properly prepare for the date. In this case, you should call her to reschedule. Women appreciate a comment as simple as "I'm not having the greatest day, and I want to be at my best when I see you. Can we reschedule? You choose the day."

Don't think you won't get a second chance. By canceling you can actually improve your standing in her eyes. Remember Mack commandment 1: "Flee and they will follow— follow and they will flee." Women are used to being pursued, not rebuffed. By rescheduling you're saying to her, "I'm patient. I can wait for this."

A final word on first dates, or any date for that matter: be cool, casual, and keep your emotions in check. If the date didn't meet your expectations, don't sweat it. Set up another date with her and make the next one better, or move on to another prospect. If the date goes well, give yourself a pat on the back—but don't get overconfident and forget your M.A.C.K. Tactics. The next time you see her, stick with the strategies and principles that have gotten you this far.

17

Wolves

No matter how tight your tactics are, there's an element we all have to deal with in social environments: other men who want what you're after. We call them Wolves.

When the average guy is out macking, he views other men as a threat. If they're hooking up with women and he's unable to, he starts feeling tense and hostile. With enough alcohol in him, he might even start a fight with the next guy who bumps into him.

This attitude is a waste of your energy and spoils your Mack mind-set. Don't look at Wolves as your enemy. You can't give off positive vibes to women, and negative vibes to men at the same time. You must erase the mentality that you're "competing" with them. You are an individual force with tactics they can't touch.

Let's say you're chatting with a girl at a club. You've decided that she's worth going for, so you offer to buy a round of drinks. She requests a vodka and cranberry. You excuse yourself to go to the bar. The club is crowded, so it takes you a few minutes to return with the drinks. When you do, another guy is talking to her.

Wack Tactic: Step in between her and the guy, give her the drink, and tell the guy, "Excuse us, we were talking." **Mack Tactic:** Say, "Excuse me," and hand her the drink: "Vodka and cranberry. That's what you wanted, right?" (showing the Wolf that you're with her). Then introduce yourself to the Wolf and shake his hand. Be friendly. Humor him for a little while; if he wants to keep trying to talk to her, let him. Be a part of the conversation. You're showing her that you don't feel threatened by another man's presence.

It's also too early for you to assume that you're the one she'd prefer to be with; she might actually be into what he's saying. (You never know; he could be a Mack, too.) If you can tell he's got game, listen to what he's saying and you might pick up a couple of pointers. Just remember, there's no sense in feeling threatened or hostile. You'll be able to tell if she'd rather return to a one-on-one convo with you.

Watch her body language. Is she giving you looks, like she wishes this guy would take a hike? If so, don't do anything about it—yet. Give him a few minutes to keep running his mouth. If he keeps standing there and won't take the hint, step closer to her. Don't put your arm around her or try to pretend that you're her boyfriend; this only makes you seem possessive. The correct tactic at this point is to ask her a direct question and resume your one-on-one convo with her, as if he isn't there.

If the guy is so dense (or drunk) that he still won't take the hint, ask her to come with you to another area of the club: "Let's go see what's going on in the other room," or "Let's go find somewhere to sit." If she wants to shed the Wolf, she'll go with you. But before you leave, give him another hand-shake and say with a friendly smile, "It was nice to meet you. Have a good night." Make it seem like you never even *considered* him to be a threat.

As you walk away with her, she might start laughing about what an idiot he was, or thank you for "saving" her. Instead of putting the guy down, say something like, "I can't blame him. Obviously I'm not the only guy here who thinks you're attractive." This demonstrates confidence. You were never worried about losing her.

A Friend to All

When a Mack enters a club, he's friendly to both men and women. If he's hanging out near some hip-looking guys, he'll introduce himself and chat with them for a few minutes. Spread positive energy. View them as your fellow man, not as competition. If you frequent certain bars or clubs, it's important to get on friendly terms with the regular patrons and the staff. When women see other people welcome you when you make your entrance, it boosts your profile.

Acting like a "tough guy" around Wolves does not impress women, at least not quality ones. They're turned off by hostile energy and don't want to be anywhere near violence. If you start arguing with a guy over her, she's likely to leave both of you in the dust. No sensible woman wants to draw that kind of negative attention.

At the same time, the Mack will always defend the honor of a woman. There are situations where you will need to assert yourself with a Wolf; if he's being disrespectful to the girl you're with, you're obligated to say something about it. The key is to keep your cool and not allow things to escalate. The calmer you remain, the more he'll look like a raving idiot. Tell him there's no excuse for the way he's behaving, that everyone here is just trying to have a good time. If there's no reasoning with him and he's spoiling for a fight, walk away with your girl. The last thing she wants is for you to start trading punches. If you're in a nightclub, it will erupt into chaos. Fighting is a sure way to ruin your night and instantly destroy any romantic bubble you've created with her.

If you're in a Wolf-heavy environment, identify "safe zones" where you can take a girl to converse with you. Don't hang around in a crowded area of a club or party trying to get to know her, while other Wolves look on. Make your intro and ask her to accompany you to a quieter area, "So I can hear what you're saying."

If a hammer enters the room—one you're interested in meeting—don't let the number of Wolves in the area affect your tempo. Don't feel that you've got to get to her before another guy does. The Mack is never in a rush. Sit back and watch while an overanxious Wolf approaches and tries to converse with her. Observe their interaction and notice the way she handles herself. Be secure in the knowledge that 90 percent of these guys are going to screw up and shoot themselves in the foot somehow. Wait for her to blow him off. Then, when you make your move a short time later, your M.A.C.K. Tactics approach is going to seem even more original and interesting by comparison.

Remember the saying, "The early bird gets the worm, but the second mouse gets the cheese." Let a Wolf walk into the trap, then move in and scoop up your cheese.

18

The World Is Yours

We've reached the end of this journey. The next time you leave your house, there should be a new stride in your step. A new tone in your voice. You're dressed for macking success, looking every bit as sharp as you feel. You project a more confident, relaxed vibe that your buddies notice and women respond to.

In other words, we'd like to officially welcome you to the Mack Militia.

You now realize the value in introducing yourself to new women every day. It's something you look forward to; batting practice makes every outing an adventure, whether it's taking a few moments to get to know your waitress, or chatting with the cute salesgirl about her opinion on new fashions. At parties, you're not anxious to meet the hottest girl in the room; you're engaging all different types of women in friendly conversations. You're constantly sending out positive energy, and you feed off the positive energy that you get in return.

When you do come across a hammer, you introduce yourself with confidence, knowing that you will engage her in a fun, stimulating conversation that transcends the usual small talk. Instead of worrying about how she'll judge you, you maintain the mind-set that the ball is in *your* court.

You put her in a comfort zone. You make her smile. You make her think. You use creative phrasing with your questions and listen, gathering intel and deciding whether this is someone you want to pursue a relationship with. If so, you've got the skills and the knowledge to make it happen. If you detect serious red flags, you'll excuse yourself with the utmost courtesy and move on to other possibilities. As a Mack, there is a *world* of possibilities out there for you to explore.

And if you're a female who's reached this final chapter, you're also going to be more confident and informed in social environments. The next time a man approaches you or takes you on date, you'll know the moves that are Mack or Wack—and be able to determine whether he's got his act together, or whether he needs to pick up this book. *M.A.C.K. Tactics* isn't about teaching guys the quickest route to your bedroom. It's about shedding the anxieties, dropping the facades, and vibing together in fun, original ways. A man who masters these lessons is a man you will enjoy spending time with. Where it goes from there is up to you.

In our next M.A.C.K. Tactics installment, we'll delve into more advanced strategies. You can always keep building upon the foundation that this book has given you. No matter how tight your tactics may be, never think there isn't room for improvement. Michael Jordan didn't become the greatest athlete in history by resting on his laurels. He was constantly searching for new ways to improve his game, whether it was defense or three-point shooting. In his prime, Jordan was unstoppable on offense; that alone would have guaranteed him a spot in the Hall of Fame. But he pushed himself to become the ultimate *complete* player.

The Mack maintains the same mentality. Beyond the bars and nightclubs, he learns how to approach and engage women in *any* environment, at any time of day. And beyond his success with women, he strives to achieve more in his professional life and form stronger relationships with *everyone* who matters to him.

We encourage you to take these tactics and make them your own. As you find which techniques work best for you, you'll be able to put your own spin on them. Many of the tactics become even more effective if you tweak them to suit your personality. Create hypotheticals. Figure out new places to take your dates. Develop new conversational topics that emphasize your good qualities and keep the dialogue flowing. Learn how to become the best possible wingman to your buddies, and show them the right way to back you up. And use the principles of negotiation not only with women, but with your boss, your coworkers, in *any* situation where demands are involved. Rack up those IOUs!

The most important thing is to get out there and start doing it. So what are you waiting for? The world is yours. It's time to put down this book, check in with the man in the mirror, and become the Mack you were born to be.

About the Authors

Rob Wiser is a native of New York City and is now a resident of Las Vegas. A graduate of New York University's film program, his screenwriting credits include *Snipes,* a crime thriller starring hip-hop superstar Nelly. When he's not traveling the globe in search of adventure and inspiration, he writes for magazines including *FHM, Cigar Aficionado, Casino Player, Hard Rock Magazine*, and *VEGAS*.

Christopher Curtis was born and raised in Queens, New York. At seventeen, he joined the Marines and was stationed at embassies in Venezuela, Yugoslavia, and Paraguay. Upon his return to the United States, he earned a degree in criminal justice and joined the Las Vegas police force, where he entered the field of hostage negotiations. After serving in countless armed and barricaded situations, he became an instructor. Currently, he is a member of the elite Crisis Intervention Team.

While making the streets safer (and being featured on occasional episodes of *Cops*), Curtis works part-time as a model and is the unofficial "Date Doctor" of the Las Vegas Metropolitan Police Force.